Diane's Story

Diane's Story

✦

From Darkness into the Light

Diane Cornelius

iUniverse, Inc.

New York Bloomington Shanghai

Diane's Story
From Darkness into the Light

iUniverse books may be ordered through booksellers or by contacting:

iUniverse
1663 Liberty Drive
Bloomington, IN 47403
www.iuniverse.com
1-800-Authors (1-800-288-4677)

Because of the dynamic nature of the Internet, any Web addresses or links contained in this book may have changed since publication and may no longer be valid.

The views expressed in this work are solely those of the author and do not necessarily reflect the views of the publisher, and the publisher hereby disclaims any responsibility for them.

ISBN: 978-0-595-48455-3 (pbk)
ISBN: 978-0-595-60549-1 (ebk)

Printed in the United States of America

Contents

CHAPTER 1   Childhood thru high school thru sophomore year 1

CHAPTER 2   Pressured into abortion, birth of my children and a
bad marriage 3

CHAPTER 3   Divorce and travel 15

CHAPTER 4   New job, hunting, and receiving a marriage
proposal. 18

CHAPTER 5   Second marriage and new husband adopting
my boys. 23

CHAPTER 6   Medical trouble while working out of town 37

CHAPTER 7   Husband working out of town, and trouble in the
neighborhood 41

CHAPTER 8   Job transfer and the birth of our first
granddaughter, and fight with Satan ending up in a
mental hospital 45

CHAPTER 9   Both of us transferred back to Baytown area and
the birth of our second granddaughter. 51

CHAPTER 10   Moved to Webster, eldest son moved back in, and
made a trip to Las Vegas 53

CHAPTER 11   Moved back to Baytown, purchased a mobile
home, birth of our grandson, and separation 54

CHAPTER 12   Purchased two acres and move the mobile home,
rededicated myself with Jesus Christ and Lord and
Savior 57

CHAPTER 13   Witnessed a miracle at the Second Baptist Church in Highlands, TX, healing of Bi-Polar Disorder by grace of God. 63

This is the story of Diane Cornelius and her rededication to our Lord Jesus Christ. Her journey in life has been filled with the love of her family and friends, but it has also taken her to many dark places. Diane has been bounded by mental illness which has challenged her along the way. She has battled with Satan while standing strong in her Christian beliefs. This story tells of her earliest memories of growing up in a large family, her marriages, the birth of her children and grandchildren and the trials and tribulations of working and raising a family while battling with Bipolar Disorder. Throughout her life Diane continued to pray to God for healing. Her prayers have been answered and she gives all glory and praise to Jesus Christ.

1

I was born in 1953 the youngest of nine siblings. I was raised in Highlands Texas. My mother always had a garden and raised chickens in a fenced area in the backyard. My family always hunted for deer and it seemed that it was a tradition that we spent the Thanksgiving holiday at a deer lease. When I was old enough to hunt and fish my dad and my brother Samuel[1] would take me with them. My other brother Dustin bought me a 4–10 shotgun and a.222 caliber rifle with a scope. This was one of the best gifts I believe that I have ever received. I fell in love with the outdoors. While growing up my family went on many vacations throughout the United States, during the spring and fall we was always going on picnics, and in the summer we spent time at the beach. As a child growing up I attended Sunday school, church and Vacation Bible School. I attended on an occasional basis. I knew Jesus as my Lord and Savior.

All of my brothers and sisters graduated from high school. Both of my brothers went to college. Throughout my school years I did well academically. The elementary school that I went to was just across the street from our house, and the junior high school was down the street. The high school I attended was in Baytown. While in school, a girl's softball league was formed and I played the first, three years that I was eligible. I was on the same first place team each year. I was the pitcher on the team and I was a good batter. My brother Samuel helped practice pitching.

I met my first love Lyle during seventh grade. Actually, I think he had me scoped out and told my friends. He was a lot of fun, but it all ended when his family moved to another city.

All my friends nicknamed me "BO" and it stayed until I graduated high school. When I began high school everything was different and I rode the bus.

---

1.   The name or names in this book were chosen at random. If any of the name or names are of the actual person or persons it is purely coincidental. The only names that are of the actual persons are those of myself and my second husband.

The school was huge with a lot more students. I kept my middle school friends and made some new ones. When my nephew Pete got his drivers license, I rode to school with him. We would go to the football games on Friday nights. After the game we would go for burgers or pizzas. We had a lot of fun.

When I was old enough to get my license, my dad told me the old family station wagon was good enough to drive to school. I organized a car pool to help pay for the gas. The old station wagon was called the "Mayflower" and the passengers were myself, Genny, Audrey, Sheena, and Leon. Of course, there was no heat or air conditioning. I used to get the biggest laugh when Genny would come walking down her driveway wrapped in a big blanket. I was working a minimum wage job at Jack-in-the-Box the latter part of my junior year.

Not too long ago my husband and I took a large amount of 8 mm film to have them put on CD's. It was wonderful to look at all the vacation coverage. These films virtually covered my whole life up through my children's second or third Christmas. I urge anyone that may have old projector film to have them converted to CD's and watch them. This is a wonderful way to visit your family history.

2

During my junior year of high school, I met the love of my life. His name was Lonnie. Lonnie has black hair, brown eyes and a brown skin color due to one of his grandmothers being an Indian. He spoke arrogantly and had a cocky walk. For awhile in junior high school he played guitar in a band. He played football at school but he quit his freshman year at Sterling high school. I met Lonnie at the Highlands Fall Carnival in 1970. I was walking and not looking where I was going. It was very crowded. When I turned around I was in his arms. He looked at me and we were locked in eye contact for several moments before he released his hold on me. We both said I know you! But I had never seen him before. There was an instant attraction there for both of us. A couple of weeks later, I saw Lonnie at his locker before first class. He asked for my phone number and walked me to my classroom. When Lonnie and I became an item we dated for eight months and I became pregnant. We really did not know what to do. We finally told his parents. Immediately Lonnie and his parents suggested that I get an abortion that this was the only solution because of our ages. I could not get Lonnie to help me tell my parents. I was angry with Lonnie because he would not go with me to tell my parents that I was pregnant. I was scared to tell them by myself. I was against the abortion from the beginning. Lonnie wanted the abortion—it was his idea. I felt so helpless and so alone that I withdrew from everyone and just did what Lonnie's parent's told me to do. I never did tell anyone in my family that I was pregnant. Lonnie's dad George asked around at his work and found the name of a doctor that knew how to perform the abortion. So Lonnie's mom Leela made an appointment for me. When I went in for the appointment Dr. Weelex examined me and told me that I would have to go to Los Angeles, California for the abortion. Abortions were illegal in Texas at this time. Dr. Weelax's associate made an appointment and travel arrangements. George and Leela paid the expenses of travel and other related expenses. The appointment was scheduled when my parents were on vacation and I would be staying at my sister Kirsten's house. George and Leela made sure that Lonnie did not come with me. I did not want to have this abortion!

The night before I was to leave for California, I made arrangements to spend the night with my friend Annis. Kirsten said she did not care as long as she had a phone number. I awoke early and left Annis' house without anyone knowing. I went to the airport and parked in a long term parking lot. I was about eleven weeks pregnant when I arrived at the clinic for the abortion. The people from the clinic was at the airport and transported everyone involved having an abortion in a van to the clinic. The clinic was a medical building. There were around fifteen to twenty teenagers there. The medical technician told everyone they would be using a new experimental drug for the anesthesia. They took us to a motel that night and the procedure was the following morning. They brought me into a room and had me put on a hospital gown. The anesthesia was given to me and it was not long before I was out. During the procedure the brightest intense white light appeared in a vision. I thought that I was dead. I knew the vision was from Jesus. The light was so bright it was very hard to see—it was blinding. I could not make out exactly what it was. I could only guess. I knew what I was doing was wrong and I had murdered my baby. After three ammonia tabs I woke up, feeling extremely bad, I could not walk without help. Immediately after the procedure as soon as they got me awoke, they sent me to the airport to go home. People from the clinic loaded all of the patients in a van. They helped me walk and off to the airport we went to go home. When I awoke, I had a very vivid memory of the vision. The vision has been burned in my memory and has stayed with me my entire life. I prayed to GOD to ask forgiveness for what I had done! From my experience I am against abortion because it is murder. You are highly emotional and it does make you physically ill after the abortion.

In 2005 (the most recent year for which there is reliable data) approximately 1.21 million abortions took place in the U. S.. From 1973 through 2005 there were more that 45 million legal abortions. 82% of all abortions are performed on unmarried women. Women between 20—24 obtained 33% of all abortions. 50% of U. S. women obtaining abortions are younger than 25. Teenagers obtained 17%. 87% of all abortions happen during the first trimester. Reported legal abortions in 2000 obtained by adolescents by age; <15—4,537; 15—8,243; 16—14,924; 17—22,535; 18—37,095; 19—44,150, with a total of 131,484 adolescents having abortions in the U. S. These are a few statistics for a more complete view http://www.cdc.gov/mmwr/preview/mmwrhtml/ss5212a1.htm or http://www.abort73.com/HTML/II-A-abortion_statistics.html.

When I arrived at the airport Lonnie was not there for me. He sent his sister Sage to take me to her house till I recovered. When my sister Kirsten did not hear from me the next day she called Annis. Annis told her I had left before she awoke and did not know where I was. Then Kirsten went to Lonnie's house and had a discussion with Leela. Whatever my sister said to Leela must have worried her immensely because Leela had Lonnie ready to ship out to her aunt and uncle's in another state. Leela was afraid because my brother-in-law was a police officer and Lonnie was under age. Then Kirsten went back a week later and talked to Leela again and the discussion must of really got heated up. Lonnie's sister Sage took me to a pay phone to call my sister. I just told Kirsten it was hard living at home with mom and dad. I asked her "Don't you remember how it was?" I told her I would be home in a couple of days.

Everything had settled down and we continued to date through high school, partying on the weekends with alcohol. During this time things seemed to be going good for us. After I graduated from high school, I worked for my brother Dustin at his business. Lonnie had a newspaper route on the weekends. He also helped his dad part-time whenever he was needed. Lonnie was drinking very heavily every weekend and usually was drunk at least one night every weekend. It was in the third week of August 1972, Lonnie and I had enough money saved to buy a new car. Lonnie's dad went with us and we bought a Chevy Nova. In August 1972, I got a good job with Southwestern Bell Telephone Company. In September 1972, Lonnie and I were married even though he was still in high school. We moved into an apartment in Baytown. Married life seemed to be going good for us. Lonnie was still drinking heavy, I was drinking also although not near as much as before. Lonnie graduated at mid term his senior year. He got a job shortly after graduating. The extra money helped greatly. We moved to Highlands and rented a mobile home. We stayed there awhile then we moved to an apartment in Houston.

Lonnie's drinking got worse. He was working the night shift and was going to work drunk occasionally. Lonnie called one night after he had went to work drunk, left work before his shift ended and got lost on his way home. I called his dad to go and find him. Lonnie had driven his car in a ditch and had to crawl out of the window.

After that things seemed to calm down for awhile. It was 1974 and we had been married for two years. I wanted a family and Lonnie did not want snotty nosed kids. I finally talked him into trying to have a baby. It had been four years since I had the abortion until now. We tried for two weeks and I went to the doctor. Well I was not pregnant. After talking to some girlfriends they suggested that

I stand on my head after sex, thinking that this would help due to my tilted uterus. We continued trying for another two weeks and back to the doctor. I went hoping for a positive pregnancy test. But the test was negative and the doctor gave me just two more weeks. If I was not pregnant by then, he said that I would not be able to have children. This news was very upsetting. I had already worn my husband out. Lonnie was not a man that could have sex every night. I got down on my knees by the bedside and prayed to GOD every night that I really wanted to have a baby before we had sex. We continued trying for those last two weeks with me hurrying to stand on my head.

I was nervous when I went back to the doctor for the test, but so elated that the test was positive. I was so happy and I rushed to my mom's house to tell her. It was very disappointing to me when she did not seem to be excited for me. She wanted us to wait a few years before having children.

We moved into a two bedroom apartment within the same complex. Everything was going fine now. Lonnie found another job and he was a lot happier. The drinking was mainly confined to the weekends. As soon as we had a down payment we bought our first house in Highlands. We did not stay there very long. Lonnie made a deal with one of his co-workers to swap our house for a small mobile home and cash. The mobile home was in the same town in a trailer park.

I had one week off of work before the expected delivery of my baby. Labor pains began during the middle of the week so off to the hospital we went. But to our dismay we were sent home, I was having false pains. Then the morning of the due date, labor pains began. These were real pains this time so we rushed to the hospital. After they got me back and prepped me I was ready for this baby now! Accept the baby was having problems, he needed to be turned so the head would come out first. Now this is where I came into play. With every contraction I would lift my knees to my chest holding them with my arms and pushing as hard as I could. This went on constantly for ten hours. Somewhere in there they induced labor. Then the next thing I knew I got a saddle-block and my baby was born. The doctor just put him on my stomach. I had a boy. Then the nurse came for him. After the doctor had finished with me, a nurse took me to my room. Lonnie and his mom were waiting for me there. They were both excited, his mom was disappointed that he did not have brown eyes and black hair like her son. Our son had blue eyes and brown hair like me.

I received a call from my work group saying good job. It was good to hear some friendly voices. The nurse brought me a huge tray of food and I ate everything. I had forgotten that I had not eaten all day. Then they brought the baby in and that is when I got such an enormous feeling of love and joy. Lonnie must of had the same emotions because he wanted to hold the baby first. Then in walks my mom, Kirsten brought her. My mom was partial to boys, she had seven girls and two boys. I thought it was very nice of my sister to bring my mom because the hospital is in Houston, about an hour trip one way. We named our baby Jay.

The first night in the hospital went well and two days later we were on our way home with our new baby boy. We first stopped off at my parent's house. DeAnn, my sister lives at home with my parents and we wanted to show her the baby. Just like my mom she instantly fell in love with my baby boy. We did not stay too long because Lonnie was working on the evening shift. When we got to the trailer it was very cold inside. Lonnie checked the thermostat and it looked fine. He had to leave for work so he called my brother Dustin to take a look at it. He had to take apart the heating unit to find what was wrong with it. Dustin found the problem and called his friend that owned the hardware store in town to meet him at the store. Stores were not open on Sunday back then. Dustin got the parts and we were nice and toasty in no time. My sister-in-law was there and she had to hold and feed the baby the whole time. I did not mind and she enjoyed every minute. I was still under the weather from ten hours of labor.

I went back to work after six weeks. Everything at home was still going along good. The baby only awoke once for feeding at night. I really liked playing with him all the time. When Jay began to crawl we really had some fun. Lonnie and his Mother found a three bedroom brick house in Baytown and he bought it. Jay was 14 months old. The house was not very well taken care of at all. DeAnn and Sarah, my sister cleaned the kitchen as best as it was going to get. It was a cold house with no insulation. We moved in and things were good. We put a new roof on the house and put insulation in the attic. At my work, things were not so good. Management promoted a black female over all of our positions. The person that was in that position had received a promotion. Suzy the new boss made it her mission to make me miserable. I was blamed for everything that was wrong in the office even to the point why nobody could get along and work together.

A year and three months after the birth of our Jay we were ready to have another child. Lonnie was a good parent. I waited a couple of weeks before going to the doctor where he confirmed that I was pregnant.

One thing both my husband and I had noticed that Jay only wanted me to carry him. Well, we were getting ready for another child. Not knowing if it will be a girl or a boy. My mom was once again uneasy with us having another baby. The nine months seem to fly by. The people that I worked with called me the "Blimp" because I had gained so much weight. I worked up to one week before the due date. After two weeks of nothing happening the doctor put me in the hospital and induced labor. But to my dismay the baby's head was not in position. So back to the pushing during contractions, but before that as the nurses were getting me ready. They had to break my water three times. They were all a-buzz about that. Around four o'clock the nurses ask another OB-GYN to look at me and he said a 'C' section was needed now! Although this was suggested my doctor was not there. They had already induced labor thru-out the day. A total of three times. With this normal delivery in process we continued. I got the saddle-block, one nurse was on one side of me and another on the other side. They were pushing on my stomach just as hard as they could to get the baby out. As soon as the baby was delivered all the nurses moved hurriedly over to a work table. I asked what the baby was and they said that I had a boy. I labored for twelve hours. We named him Joel.

I looked to see him and he was all black and blue. I can not exactly remember when or who told me that the umbilical cord was wrapped around his neck three times. He was being choked upon delivery. I did need a 'C' section after all. Anyway, they shaved his hair and put in IV's and kept him in an incubator for four days. I stayed in bed all day, then the next day I got a handicap walker. I had to go see my baby. It was a long way to the nursery, but I made it. It was such a shock to see your baby attached to all those IV's. I had to go real slow back to my room because I was so weak. I do not remember Lonnie being there after delivery. The next time I remember seeing him was the day both Joel and I was released from the hospital. We went to my mom's house because she had Jay. My mom was just so proud to see Joel she had been worrying about him also. It was good to see Jay he had missed me and I surely missed him. We decided that my mom would keep Jay for awhile till I got back on my feet a little better. Everything was great Jay came home and our whole family was together.

After two weeks of the birth of our second son we decided to build a three car garage. It sounded like a good idea, but Lonnie wanted to build it ourselves. So here I am just two weeks out of the hospital out spreading cement. After about three months we had a finished garage.

Joel was having ear infections that would not heal. He was keeping us up a lot at night. I was using a pediatrician that my mother-in-law used, but he was not clearing his infection. I found a pediatrician in Baytown. He gave him fourteen days of antibiotics instead of what the other doctor was giving him. In two weeks we had a happy boy again.

Things now at work were heating up, between sleepless nights, very nervous, irritable, lost a lot of weight, and a supervisor that was giving reverse discrimination to me. Jay was 2 1/2 years old and Joel was 6 months old. After several months of that I had a break-down and admitted myself into a mental hospital. I did not like the choice of medication I was put on. When it was time for the medication everyone would line-up at the nurses' station which was about twenty-five to thirty feet long. The nurse would hand out cups and everyone would start pounding those cups on the counter. I want to tell you I wanted out of there. Come to find out the nurse was putting Thorazine (psychotic drug) in everyone's cup. I still was not sleeping good even in there. They had me take some test, but I just put down anything. I did not want to play any mental games. They came down one night and woke me and were putting men's pajamas on me. I had my own pajamas on. I took them off and walked to where dirty sheets go and threw them in. And in a few minutes the door to my room opened and the pajamas were tossed in. So, I got back up and walked back down the hall and tossed them back in the dirty laundry. I did not have anymore problems after that. My brother Samuel and his wife came and visited with me, it was great to see him. I did not get to see him very much, he lives in another state. One night while at the hospital there was a bad storm with a lot of rain. There was a great deal of damage to the hospital.

When I was released from the hospital Lonnie took me to stay at his mom's house. I do not know why he did not take me to my mom's house. There was something wrong with the medication Thorazine I was taking. I was swelling, had a rash over my entire body, and I itched like crazy. I told Lonnie and he told his mom and they did nothing. I could not sleep at night because I was itching so badly. I only had to stay there a couple of nights and then we went home. I finally convinced Lonnie that something was wrong that the swelling and the itching was not normal and he took me to a doctor. The doctor put me in the hospital and ran all kinds of tests. They found out that I was allergic to Iodine—that is why I could not take the Thorazine and I had sugar diabetes. The doctor told my husband that I needed to see a psychiatrist. We went home. I was put on sugar diabetes pills and a diet.

By this time we were having marital problems and were not getting along very well. I made Lonnie take me to my mom and dad's house. It was now that I told my parents that while in high school that I had an abortion. They did not have too much to say but Lonnie was extremely upset that I told them. We only stayed there for about an hour so I could tell my parent's and visit with my boys.

My mom was keeping the kids for me while I was getting adjusted to the diabetes and new psychotic medication. When Lonnie worked the day shift I would go over and stay with my mom also. I talked with Sarah explaining to her that I was not getting better. I did not like the psychiatrist and Lonnie was taking me back to the hospital. Lonnie was angry I told my parents about the abortion and thought I was acting irrational. I was angry with him because he could not stand behind his wedding vows—in sickness and health. She reassured me just to go along with everything and when I got out I could stay with her and her husband. Sarah would find me another doctor.

Well, as it went I had a bad dream (I think it was a bad dream—I do not remember). Lonnie asked me if I remembered him slapping me real hard in the face trying to wake me up. I did not. I was in a black-out. During the black outs I would speak out but do not remember anything about what I was dreaming nor saying. Whatever I must have said upset him and in the morning, Lonnie just packed my bag. He told me that he was taking me to the hospital and I was making him drag me to the vehicle, clinging to each porch post along the way. I could not understand why since just two weeks prior I had been in the hospital for tests. These concluded that I was diabetic. I guess I will never understand being put in a mental hospital for one bad dream and I was sleeping every night. Normally patients are not hospitalized unless they are not sleeping. They put me in a room when I got there and then they put me in a different room with a black woman. This woman was a very angry person and no one wanted to be around her. The nurses were trying to play games, but within a day she and I were best friends and she did not want me to move to another room. She just hugged me to the surprise of the nurses. A day later the staff wanted to move me to a different room. When the tech and I looked thru all the baggage. There was no suitcase for me to put my clothes in. Lonnie had taken me to the hospital, took all my clothes out of the suitcase and left with the suitcase. That definitely sent a message. Then Sarah my sister told me Lonnie took our children to my mom's for her to keep them. When my mom asked about me he said that "I have her exactly where I want her"! This upset everyone in my whole family. I do not remember how long I stayed in the hospital. I am thinking about two or three weeks. Kirsten brought my mom and my children to see me one afternoon. This lifted my spirits immensely.

Lonnie was there when I was released from the hospital to pick me up. He took me straight to Sarah's home. Lonnie was staying there too. My sister Sarah made an appointment with a psychiatrist in Baytown. Sarah took Lonnie and me for the first appointment which was an hour long. Dr. Wren talked to both of us first. Then he asked me to step outside leaving Lonnie talking to the doctor. After awhile Lonnie came out and I was called back in. Lonnie did not like this at all. He wanted to have control over me and what I told the doctor. This doctor was there to take care of me and I liked that. The doctor got me on the correct medication. I liked this doctor and was convinced that I would get better. Dr. Wren told me that the medication that I had been put on (Thorazine) just makes you a zombie and how can you treat a zombie? I told him that I was allergic to iodine and really had a bad reaction to it. I began to feel better on the new medication. After about two weeks Sarah and her husband could tell that I was real nervous around Lonnie so they asked him to move out. I really felt at ease and no pressure on me after Lonnie moved out. I do not exactly remember how long it was before I went back to work. I did get to spend time with my children at mom's. I remember going to our family Christmas breakfast. I had taken my medication before leaving Sarah's house and after not eating in about an hour I was having problems. I went out to the car with the shakes bad and could barely talk. What surprised me was that one of my nephew's wife followed me and I could not explain to her what was happening to me. I managed to tell her to get Sarah. We left and after awhile at Sarah's house I was able to eat and started to feel better.

I went back to work in about five months after my medication was regulated. There was a new boss over the office now. After a couple of days, my boss wanted me to go to San Antonio for a couple of days to explain the computer system to them. It was fun to get away. When I came back, I took a taxi from the airport to my mom's house. Lonnie was there. He said that he had found a house there in town and wanted me to look at it with him. Lonnie wanted us to get back together. The house was just nine months old and in fantastic condition. Three bedroom brick house with a two car garage. Lonnie talked me into buying it. We moved in and everything was going good.

During our marriage we went on four or five vacations to his aunt and uncle's in another state. Then even George and Leela moved to another state. They did not stay too long and they moved back. We had a cab-over camper on our truck. One summer, my mom and dad left a couple of days ahead of us. They took Jay and Joel in their motor home and of course DeAnn was there too. We were all heading to the mountains. It was fun with a campfire at night. The nights were cold. Before Jay was born Lonnie bought a boat. I remember only using the boat once on a camping trip.

Lonnie bought my brother-in-law Howard's 1967 Chevelle SS one year. He put everything he could buy on it to make it go faster. Then one night on his way home from work he was racing and he blew something up on it, so he sold it.

I had a check-up with my OB-GYN and he did not believe I had sugar diabetes and he wanted to retest me. I did not jump up and down and agree because it was a hard test to go thru. But I said O.K. Dr. Parik called a couple of days later while I was at work and the test was negative. I was very elated to hear those words, I even think I asked him twice. I continue to test for diabetes, and to this day, I am happy to say that I have not had to go back on the diabetic medication.

Work was not going so well for me. While I was gone the company had upgraded to a newer computer which is good for the company. Although for me it was not because, I was finding it extremely difficult to do my job due to not being familiar with this system. My supervisor thought I knew how to do my job on the new computer system and I did not. Because of the changes and not knowing the systems, I started missing a lot of work. After awhile of this Lonnie told me to give the company my two week notice and quit. So, I did give my notice after working there for six years. For the next two weeks everything was great, the boys were well adjusted to our new home. One evening, Lonnie's youngest sister came over and everyone was hungry. So, I fixed a meal which included pork chops, mashed potatoes, green beans, and rolls. I had just finished placing everything on the table, everyone was seated and Lonnie came home. He was very upset that I had fixed this meal. He was always on some kind of crazy diet to lose weight. Lonnie did not think of anyone but himself, not our children, his sister, or me.

After two weeks of being unemployed Lonnie told me that I would have to find a job because he could not pay the bills just on his salary. I looked around and found a minimum wage job and he was satisfied. I enjoyed this job, but it was kind of depressing that I left a good paying job just two weeks earlier for a minimum wage job. I worked there for six months. While I was working there I had taken a couple of days off and Lonnie and I took the kids over to my mother's house for a few days. Then we loaded up our cab over camper and headed for New Mexico for a skiing trip. We had never skied before. We took some lessons. Towards the end of the lessons my feet got cold. We went into the lodge to warm-up. After the little break, off to the ski lifts we went. We were supposed to get off half way up the mountain, but there were no signs. We saw a hut with an Indian in it. Lonnie jumped off the lift. I could not move that quickly and when I finally jumped, I ended up in a snow drift about waist deep. The Indian in the hut just shook his finger at me. It took awhile for me to get out of the snow drift. Once I finally did, I looked around I could not find Lonnie and I did not know which trail he had taken to the lodge. I took the trail that the most skiers were on. Well this was a bad idea. I was looking for a beginners trail and I was on an intermediate trail. Everyone was flying by me so fast I was scared. I tried to stay real close to the trees and the whole course was nothing but a mixture of snow and ice. I do not know how but I finally made it to the lodge. I will never go back to that resort again not unless they get more snow.

We returned home from vacation and everything was going well. Late one afternoon, I decided to go for a bowl of chili. Lonnie was at work. The kids were at my mom's house. It had been a while since I had ridden my motorcycle so I took it to the restaurant. When I arrived I unfortunately parked in a hole. The bike started to tip over and before I knew it the bike and I were on the ground. I picked it up and tried to start it without any luck. I checked the bike over making sure that the kill switch was in working order and it was. I tried a few more times to start it with no success. I went on in the restaurant and got the chili. After eating, I made another attempt to start the bike, still without success. I called Lonnie and told him what had happened. He was angry, because he would have to find someone to come with him to get me and the bike. He said that he would call his mother, but this would be a great inconvenience to her. She arrived and when we were about half way home I felt like I was going to throw up. Before I had time to tell her to pull over up it came. I had on a big jacket so I threw up on my shirt and zipped up my jacket. When I arrived home I went in and took a shower with my clothes on to clean up and then I washed my clothes. To this day I hear that his mom thinks I am a bad woman for throwing-up on my shirt.

I thought that everything with our marriage was going fine. When Lonnie would get off of the evening shift he would go bowling till about three in the morning. I really did not think much of this, it was giving him something to do beside just going to work and then coming home to me and the kids. After a couple of months, Lonnie came home one night around three in the morning and woke me up and told me to pack all my clothes and the kids clothes and get out by morning. I asked him why? He said that the boys left a toy by the front door and for me to come and look. It was a match box toy car left by the hallway entrance about three inches from the wall. He is kicking us out because of one toy! Come morning, the boys and I went to my mom's house. Lonnie could never accept me being sick and not working. Lonnie was more into materialistic items than raising a family. Lonnie stayed at the house for awhile and then put it up for sale when he moved out. Sheena, a friend and I moved in until it sold. We stayed there about a month, then it sold and we had to move.

From the sale of the house we cleared eighteen thousand dollars. Lonnie took my portion, nine thousand dollars and bought a two bedroom mobile home and had it moved to a mobile home park near my parent's house. This was just one more sign of his controlling nature. Lonnie somehow was able to finance the balance of the mobile home with a bank in town. I do not know how he did it, but

Lonnie and a banker somehow got the financing in my name. It does not make sense, how was I to make payments. I did not have a job. This really upset me, he did not even discuss if I wanted a trailer or where to put it. I would have much rather moved in with my parents until I had some time to think and get a job. I was just lost that summer. Things were happening around me, I did not have a job, I did not want the trailer and Lonnie kept sending me mixed signals. Lonnie continued to try to control my life. One week I decided to get away and give myself some space. My mom and DeAnn were keeping Jay and Joel for me while I took Sheena and her brother Beenie to Florida to Disney World. They had never been there before. After we came back home I took Sheena out of state to get her daughter.

Lonnie did not want to work towards saving the marriage and we got a divorce in 1979. The divorce was very hard on me because I did not want to have the divorce.

According to Divorcemag.com/statistics/statsUS.shtml. There were approximately 2,230,000 marriages in 2005—down from 2,279,00 the previous year, despite a total population increase of 2.9 million over the same period. The divorce rate in 2005 (per 1000 people) was 3.6—the lowest rate since 1970, and down from 4.2 in 2000 and from 4.7 in 1990. (The peak was at 5.3 in 1981, according to the Associated Press.) Median age at first marriage Males 26.9, Females 25.3. Median age at first divorce Males 30.5, Females 29. Median duration of first marriages that ended in divorce Males 7.8 years, Females 7.8 years. Median duration of second marriages that ended in divorce Males 7.3 years, Females 6.8 years.

3

In the summer of 1979, I went to the Navy Office and applied to take an entrance exam. The exam was easy. They called me for an appointment in a few days. They said "they could use me in communications on an aircraft carrier". Boot camp would be at the Great Lakes. I would have to sign my children over to someone else for Guardianship. I told them there was no way I was signing my children over to anyone and I walked out.

In late June, Annis and I thought of a trip to Bar Harbor, Maine. Her parents were enthused and wanted to come along. I was able to get my sister Kirsten to care for Joel while I was on this trip. So Annis, her son Martin, Annis' mom and dad, my son Jay and myself went to the airport and off we went. The boys were excited about the plane flight. We had stopped at a strip center in Massachusetts to do some shopping and after awhile Jay needed to go to the restroom. I asked everyone in that strip center if they had a restroom and each of them told me no. So I did the only thing I knew, being from Texas, I took him out to the rent car and told him to pee by the front tire with his back to everyone. While he was doing this a couple of gals came by screaming and hollering "you can't do that, not in the parking lot" I hollered back "none of the stores have a restroom and the boy needs to go". They just kept hollering and driving and I was so irritated I flipped them off and then they went on. Jay felt better after he relieved himself. I do not understand why stores will not let you use their facilities, I know that they have them. We were all having such a good time. Kirsten called and said that my trailer had been broken in, and that some things were stolen. With this news, I had to make arrangements for Jay and I to go back home. I had to leave on a small jet to Boston where I would fly home from there. We were going to miss the 4th of July parade in that little town we was staying in. Also, I sure missed the lobster and the clam chowder. When I arrived back home all that was gone was the stereo and some money that I had in my piggy bank. I talked with the detective and he knew who it was that had broken into my house. I did not know but when my friend Sheena who was staying with me was doing drugs and bringing men in after I had gone to bed. Shortly thereafter, I started drinking beer and Sheena talked me into trying some cocaine. All the cocaine did was just made me sober. So I never tried cocaine again.

I came home a little late one night and when I got there Sheena had two of my brother-in-laws there with her. She was sitting on Dalton's lap and Greg had a chair pulled close to them. It was all I could do to restrain myself from running over there and grabbing a hand full of hair and drag her out of the trailer. Instead, I told them I needed to be somewhere early in the morning, so they would have to leave. Dalton is my sister Laural's husband and Greg is Kirsten's husband. Sheena and I were having some difficulties with her drug use and coming in all hours of the night and the people she would have coming over after I had gone to bed. After Dalton and Greg left, I told her she was going to have to leave too.

At this point in my life I was going out with different men, it was usually for only one night.

The boys and I moved out of the trailer and moved in with my mom and dad. I rented the trailer to Kirsten's sister-n-law. I finally found a job at the paper mill, the only problem was that I would have to work shift work. The work was hard but I liked it. As with all new hires they initiated me, and they got me good. It was a lot of fun how they situated me just right to pour that bucket of water on me from above. Every evening when I got home the boys were so excited they would have me sit down and Jay and Joel would each take one of my boots off. At this time in my life, things were good. I had a job that I liked and the boys and I were a happy family. I did not have any outbreaks related to mental stress.

Later in the fall of that year, Sheena told me one day when we were still living in the house that a woman called looking for Lonnie, and she said it happened a couple of times before. So, now it all makes sense. The toy was just an excuse to kick me and the kids out. Lonnie was not man enough to tell me he had found someone else. Lonnie just blames it all on the boys. I never even once checked on him when he was bowling, maybe I should have! Come to think about it I did not even know if the bowling alleys were even open that late in the middle seventies. I was 26 years old, Jay was 4 years old and Joel was 2 years old.

After two months of working at the paper mill I was able to purchase a new Dodge truck. I called Lonnie and told him that I would not need the car. He said that his brother Percy was looking for a car. Percy took over the payments.

The divorce settlement ordered Lonnie to pay four hundred dollars child support, maintain healthcare benefits on the boys. Lonnie would get visitation every other weekend. I was stuck with paying all the bills. When we were leaving the court my attorney advised me not to pay the bills that Lonnie was just as responsible as I was for the bills. I did pay them. I called each of the creditors and explained the situation. I told them that I would send them what I could.

The boys were nervous about going with their dad. I told them that it would only be for the weekend and that they would be coming back home. They came back OK. They were excited to be back home. Lonnie kept pushing me even before the divorce to split up the boys. He wanted Joel but did not want Jay. I told him that I would never split up the boys.

To thank my mom for all of her help, I bought her a red Plymouth "K" car station wagon. I paid for it until October of 1981 when DeAnn took over payments. Mom really liked this car, it was her first car. Mom could go to the store without having to find someone to take her. She also enjoyed taking the kids to school.

4

Around November I received a call from the local telephone company (General Telephone Electronic) for an interview. I had been waiting to hear from them for awhile now. I interviewed with Jack, the supervisor over the engineering department. He asked me some questions and I told him I had previous experience with Southwestern Bell. He hired me, although I could not start for a week. I had to give the paper mill my notice of leaving. They tried to talk me out of leaving but I told them that I liked working for the phone company. I knew the job well.

The weekend before I was to start with the phone company my mom, Dad, DeAnn, Jay, Joel, and I went to the deer lease. It was opening weekend and we were all excited. Mom and I hunted together, come to think about it I believe that this was the only time we hunted together. We were sitting in a ground blind for about fifteen minutes and an eight point buck came out, I took aim and squeezed the trigger. It was a clean hit. We waited ten to fifteen minutes before we went to the deer. Mom was excited about the size of the rack. Mom was in a hurry to skin and gut him.

The first day of work at my new job was finally here. Everyone was really nice and I felt comfortable. Before long the boss was letting me go on field trips to help the techs. I was really getting to make a lot of field trips now. I was really learning new information and was adapting rapidly. I then was promoted to the next highest wage level. There was a management change Jack became a tech and Hayes was now my supervisor.

I received a letter in the mail from a collection agency. When I called them it was for the car I had given back to Lonnie. The bank had to pick it up because Percy was not making payments. The collection agency wanted $500. I told them I would pay $250 and they would have to get the rest from Lonnie. I really should not have paid anything because Lonnie took the car and it was his responsibility. I never heard from the bank again.

Since my divorce I started dating a couple of guys. All of them were short term relationships from three weeks to a couple of months. It was mostly about sex and not building a true relationship. Lonnie got married to Dora, a gal he works with.

After Kirsten's sister-n-law moved out of the trailer my dad and I made repairs. We moved the trailer on DeAnn's lot on Lake Sam Rayburn.

Hayes and I got along real well. He wanted to go to our families deer sausage making party. I had to get permission from whosever house is hosting. Hayes and I were put on the grinder. I was loading the meat and he was operating the manual grinder and drinking beer whenever we had a chance. When it came time to grind Kirsten's meat, there was a lot of hair in it. Hayes and I were trying to pick it out. When her husband Greg saw us picking it out he said go ahead and grind it that Kirstin will never know. So, Hayes and I looked at each other took a big gulp and started grinding. A great deal of work goes into making sausage, but everyone had a good time.

My mom would make a big pan of homemade biscuits and I would cook them in the oven at work. That is what we would have for morning break. She did not do it all the time, but she just liked to bake.

Our department was changing. Two guys, Ollie and Perceval, from the northern states came in replacing two people who retired. In addition, two local clerks, Meg and Kelley were hired. Meg, Kelly, and I hit it off right away. Other changes were being made too. Facility techs were added to the engineering department.

One day while I was on a field trip with Cory, an outside plant tech he was really worried about his son. He was not happy with his son's living arrangements. I told Cory if his son does not mind going out with someone that is older than him that I would go on a date with him. In about a week right about quitting time, in walks a guy with a cowboy hat and a woman. They went to Cory's desk. I figured out that this must be his son and Cory's wife. When four o'clock came I left. I had gotten my income tax check and I was going to go to the bank and pay off my truck. Cory's son followed me outside and introduced himself as Hugh. It just happened I was on my motorcycle that day and I was having trouble getting it to start. He asked if he could try. I said "go ahead" he was able to get it started, but he would not take no for an answer of not seeing me the rest of the afternoon. I told him what I had to do and he told me he would take me, then afterwards we could go do something. Hugh followed me home to drop off the motorcycle. I told my mom where I was going and introduced her and the boys to Hugh. We went to the bank not far from where Hugh lives and I got my business completed. We went to a small beer joint near by and played pool and drank a couple of beers. I beat Hugh in two games of pool and he made me promise never to tell his dad. He had me back home early and asked me out for the next night, I said OK.

I did not know what was going on, but there was a big commotion going on with Cory the next day at work. He talked to me in the parking lot and asked if Hugh went home after he left my house. I told him, I guess he did. He told me, that old gal he is living with is raising hell because he did not come home last night. In a little while Cory told me that he stayed the night at his sister's house.

When it came time for our date Hugh would not tell me where we were going. I soon found out—seafood, shrimp, oysters, or whatever you wanted he said. I do not remember what I ordered, I had a very good time. Hugh could put away food so fast, just watching him was comical. On the way home he asked me to go out on a date the next night; again I told him yes.

At work the next day, Hugh was giving all his guns to Cory out in the parking lot. They were putting them in Cory's vehicle.

When we left for our date Hugh headed straight for the seafood restaurant. Once again the food was delicious. I had come to the conclusion Hugh was getting serious. Sitting in his truck in the driveway at my mom's, we were talking and he tells me about the gal he was living with, but she is gone now. We embraced and kissed and I thought to myself he just might be the one. Before he left he asked me out again for the next night.

Work was just work, Kelly, Meg, and I were having a good time. I had put in a bid for a tech position. Not only would this position increase my salary, but I would have the opportunity of increasing my work knowledge and this excited me.

Hugh again headed for the seafood restaurant. As usual the food was great. Hugh showed me the chemical plant he was working at as a contractor on the way home. We arrived at my mom's house and in the driveway we kissed and hugged. Then he asked me out again for another date for the next night, again I said yes.

When Hugh came to get me for our date this time, I got in the truck and told him "look you have taken me three nights for seafood—I know the hamburgers have to start", he just laughed and said "you are right".

Back at the job, I was having problems with Perceval and Ollie staring at me all the time. Their desks were facing mine. Day in and day out I was getting very nervous. I thought that I would gross them out by picking a small scab I had on my arm and put it in my mouth. Later, when Ollie became my supervisor, he made me sign a letter stating that I had done that and the letter was placed in my personnel file. I kept it in my mouth for awhile and then got up and walked away from my desk and spit it out. That did not work, all I heard was "that is disgusting".

Hugh and I were going dancing on the weekends now, he knows how to dance very well. Jay and Joel were getting attached to him also.

I cooked a meal for Hugh at his rent house one night. If I remember right it was smothered steak, mashed potatoes and green beans. That was the night Hugh decided he would not let me go. We made love for the very first time and he was what I needed. I fell in love with him that night.

Hugh was making a couple of trips to my mobile home on DeAnn's lots for the weekend at Lake Sam Rayburn.

On some weekends a whole group of us would go dancing on Friday nights. I remember Meg because she would dance with Hugh when I wanted to sit for awhile. It felt good to have met some new friends that liked to go dancing. A couple of guys from the crew, Barnard and Norman started going out dancing also.

Hugh had to change jobs and started contracting at a different plant. He would come straight to my house everyday after work, but I noticed he had a six pack of beer before he made it here. I thought to myself not again. Drinking had been a major problem in my previous relationship. But he was different, somehow right then it did not matter. I was washing his clothes for him on Saturday's and when a five dollar bill was left in the wash he told me to keep it. Now, that impressed my mom. She knew how close Hugh and I were getting and she did not want to let go of Jay and Joel.

Hugh's aunt Alethia had an empty house and he asked her if he could rent it, so they made a rental agreement. We started cleaning the place up spic and span. On a July afternoon we were moving Hugh out to the rent house. We were sitting on the couch in the back of the truck when he asked me "what would you say if I asked you to marry me". I did not answer him right away. I told him "I guess you will have to ask me to find out"! Then he asked "will you marry me"? I said yes. We unloaded the truck thinking we would go to a movie, but it had begun to drizzle and then rain on the metal roof. We were both so tired we just sat on the bed and the next thing we knew it was almost dark. Hugh did not go stay there right away or even talk to his aunt, but when it came time for us to move in we went there and she was renting the house to someone else. I got my mop, broom, and dust pan back, but Hugh lost all his furniture.

The whole family made a trip to the mall, mom, DeAnn, Hugh, Jay, Joel and I. The mall was fairly new and not all the stores were open yet. Hugh and I were there to buy our wedding rings. We found and bought what we wanted and were just exiting the store when we heard a lot of glass breaking. We turned around and some guys were taking jewelry out of the showcases and started running shooting their guns and Hugh took off after them. I asked him when he got back "what do you want to do get shot?" He did not say anything. DeAnn said "this is all wrong, you are not meant to be together". I told her it is only a robbery, it is nothing to do with us.

At work, Perceval moved to Dickinson and Ollie moved to a desk by Hayes. Talk about dancing a jig, I did not have those bozo's staring at me all day anymore!

About a year and a half after we divorced, Lonnie was sending papers wanting to take me back to court. He wanted the kids longer in the summer and Christmas, and on Fathers day. He was still pushing to break up the kids and get Joel. When I countered back for more child support, Lonnie dropped his pursuit in this matter.

5

All our friends were planning a camping trip to New Braunfels on August 21–23, 1981. I remember Meg, Kelly, Ami, Phil, Norman, and Barnard were all there.

Hugh and I took off work the Friday of August 21, 1981, because we went to downtown Houston to get our marriage license, then walked across the street to the Justice of the Peace's office to get married. On the way over to the J. P's office I turned to Hugh and told him if he wanted out now was the time. He said that he was not backing out and we were married. Before leaving Houston we stopped at the bank where his truck was financed and made a payment. We left and were heading out of Houston, I was starting to get a sinus headache. We stopped in Seguin for the night. We consummated our marriage. My headache was getting worse. Hugh left to find some medicine. He returned with the medicine. I took it and he watched football the rest of the evening. I think that the Rams and the Chargers were playing that night; although I am not sure who won. What a honeymoon me with a sinus headache and Hugh watching football.

The next morning my headache had eased, so we decided to go find the group. We found them way down the river and we told them that we were married. Now we had something to party about. I remember the water was so cold that I had to drink a couple of beers just to get in the water. We all had inner-tubes to ride on down the river and we had one tube with an ice chest full of beer in it. After a couple of hours riding down the river Kelly got caught in some long hanging branches and fell out of her tube, her bathing suit top came off. Hugh was right there holding her inner-tube with his mouth wide open and Barnard jumped off of his tube and picked her up and put her back in her inner-tube. During all of this she managed to keep her bathing suit top and she put it back on. We stayed on the river all that day having a great time.

We camped at a campground that night with the group. We went to bed early because of my headache and a little too much sun. We wanted to get an early start home in the morning.

We did not tell our parents when we came home that we had gotten married. I did not want to upset my mom by taking the kids from her right away. Jay was four and Joel was two when Lonnie and I divorced. Now Jay six and Joel four, and I had been staying at my mom's house for two years. I wanted to gently take them away from her. We started taking the boys everywhere we went. The whole group would meet at Barnard and Norman's condo every Monday night and make chili. We would watch football and drink beer. We looked around and found an apartment in the same complex that Barnard and Norman were living at, but it would not be ready until Oct. 1. We still had to find a bedroom suite for us and the boys, the living room furniture, kitchen table and chairs and everything that goes in the kitchen.

It was not long before moving day was here and the whole group helped and Hayes even showed up. Mom made a big BBQ lunch for everyone to eat. The moving was easy. The hard part was having a place for everything. The boys were a little confused so I told them just to stay at my mom's house because everything was a mess.

On one of Lonnie's weekends to keep the boys, we met him at the store before you come into the complex. On this particular time he took the boys on Friday night. Hugh and I were about to have dinner on Saturday night, Lonnie calls and says he was bringing Jay back home. He did not give an explanation or anything he just dropped him off. Jay was just as happy as he could be because Hugh and I were having a candlelight dinner. Jay never told me what happened to make him come home early.

I am now going to speed the story up here. I found out in 2005 from Joel that Dora, Lonnie's wife would make Jay and Joel stay in a room and not come out until Lonnie got home from work. They would have to stay as the boy put it "locked" in a room until their daddy came and let them out. They would be in there for eight hours not counting his drive time to and from work. Judgment day is coming. Jay never went with his daddy again.

In November 1981, there was some scurrying around at work and I found out that they made Barnard a tech. So, I go right up to Hayes and tell him I have a bid in for a tech and I have more seniority than Barnard. I made the statement "Do I need to file a grievance?" He said "hold on, I did not know you wanted the job. Let me check everything" He came back in awhile and said that there were two openings. The test date would be in a couple of days. On the test date, I was not too nervous because I had passed the one for Southwestern Bell. During the test, Barnard was making all kinds of goofy noises and I thought something was wrong with him. I just ignored him and concentrated on my test. Lea was the personnel clerk giving us the test. The test was very long and I thought it would never end. It finally did and I knew that I had passed. Lea asked me to stay a minute, she wanted to know if all that noise was coming from Barnard. I told her that I did not know, I just tried to ignore it. She told me that if I ever had trouble with any of the men to talk to her boss Miss Armstrong the Personnel Director. I just told her OK.

The next week I received a call from the personnel director's office. Miss Armstrong wanted to talk to me about Barnard and his making all those noises during the test. I just told her that I ignored him. Then she wanted to know if he had ever made any sexual advances towards me and I told her that he had not. She said that she was not going to let things get out of hand around here.

We had a very special Christmas for the boys this being our first together. The boys were at my mom's house Christmas Eve, while Hugh and I were putting things together including a pup tent in the living room. That sounds easy but it took most of the afternoon. Then we placed all their gifts in it. After our family Christmas breakfast, one of our family traditions, we went back to the apartment. All the work that Hugh and I did was worth every minute when we saw the look on those two little boys eyes get big and round. They asked if we were going to camp out. We told them sure they can. So they camped out in the living room for a couple of days. Then they moved into their bedroom. From that point on, they stayed with us. I would have to get up a little earlier in the mornings to take the boys over to my mom's house before work. I would pick them up after work.

We only stayed in the apartment for six months. We bought a very small house in Highlands. Just before we moved in Hugh ripped out all of the walls and installed insulation and put up new paneling. It had two bedrooms, living room, kitchen, and a bath. The boys had a huge back yard to play in now. We did not have enough money for the down payment, so my sister Esther loaned us the amount we needed. It was owner financed by two women, Vera and Joy. The payments were low which was good for us. The hot water heater was bad so we had to buy a new one. Sarah's husband Lawrence helped us install it. When we had enough money we purchased a new washer, dryer, two ton air conditioner, and a heater large enough that would heat the whole house. We did not have a pantry so Hugh built one on rollers. He also rebuilt the kitchen sink and made the kitchen counter in an "L" shape that gave me more room.

It was shortly after moving in that I had an appendectomy in the first part of 1982. I only stayed in the hospital a couple of days.

Hugh had a bass boat. Coming in from one of our fishing trips he backed the boat trailer up and drove the boat on it. He told me to pull the truck up. I had not driven his truck that much, when I let off of the clutch and gave it some gas to my surprise I had it in reverse and backed it in the water. He yelled, "STOP STOP". When I stopped he jumped out of the boat and pulled it out. I had backed the truck up far enough for the water to get over the rear tires and in the bed of the truck. He said "I can not believe you backed my truck into the bay." Oops!

Hugh was having a hard time finding and keeping a job. He would work for awhile then get laid off due to contract jobs ending. To help I worked part-time at Jack-in-the-Box after my full time job. It got so bad and he was so frustrated I told him maybe me and the boys should leave. He went ballistic, he rammed his head against the door jam and then headed for the front door. He broke it right in two. I just told him that was very foolish that you will have to fix it right now. Towards the summer, I got a call from my lawyer while I was working at Jack-in-the-Box. He told me that Lonnie's lawyer had called him and said that Lonnie wanted to give up his parental rights. I asked him why and he said he really did not know. That was it for me. I told the boss I needed to go home with some very important news. Everyone was so happy. Hugh had wanted to adopt the boys.

When it came court time for Hugh to adopt the boys, he and I were there with our attorney along with the attorney representing the boys. The judge goes thru the procedure and tells me that if Hugh and I were to get a divorce that he could get custody of the kids because he would have full parental rights. Then we go on to name them Jay Cornelius and Joel Cornelius. The last thing the judge harshly barked out was that Lonnie from this day forward was a stranger on the street and nothing more, just a stranger. The boys adjusted very well to the adoption.

Hugh was still unable to find a job so our only decision was for him to join the Army. I had to have him at the Federal Building in Houston at 5 am on August 26, 1982. It was hard splitting up but I did not know how hard till after Hugh had gotten out and I was circling the building. I heard somebody crying. I asked what is wrong. Jay said "I already lost one daddy, now I am losing another". I told him that he was not losing him. He is just going off to work for the Government. He will be back.

When I returned back to work, I found out that I was scheduled for a three week OPT school in San Angelo. Justin, Ollie's buddy from up north was scheduled also. He had transferred here as a field drafter. We had an instructor that made it enjoyable. The weeks did not fly by but the weather was nice. I passed all the tests required to pass the course. I learned how to design communication cables.

Hugh was getting along in the Army. I guess that I should not have told him about Jay making the comment about losing a daddy. This upset Hugh and he lost his main focus. I also wrote his Commanding Officer about getting him out of the Army. Hugh was released within a month. He received an Honorable Discharge.

We went to Kountze to buy a used travel trailer from Willy, a guy that had retired from where I worked. It took most of the day, he lived way down in the woods. We used the trailer at a hunting lease one season in Red Land. Every time it rained the trailer leaked bad. That season Hugh killed an eight point whitetail deer so I guess all was not lost on the trailer.

I came down with an upper-respiratory infection and was hospitalized at Gulf Coast Hospital. Dr. Braff was attending to me. That first night was bad every time they turned my IV on to let the medicine into my veins, I would immediately start throwing up. I would call the nurse she would shut the IV off. Then come back a little later and turn it on again and I would start throwing up again. I called the nurse again, she shut it off. I asked her to call Dr. Braff. She said that she would not do that he was already asleep, we can not disturb him. I told her not to turn that IV on again. The next day Dr. Braff came in and I told him I would throw up every time the IV was started. He changed the medication and everything was fine. He said he was also going to release me to the mental health part of the hospital because I was having problems and not sleeping at night. I would be seeing Dr. Wren. I stayed in the hospital for about three weeks in the mental health group. I was diagnosed with nervous exhaustion and placed back on medication to help relieve the nervousness.

Hugh finally landed a steady contract job. Along this time I had to have a partial hysterectomy in 1983. This knocked me off of my feet for awhile. Dr. Parik was my doctor and he was the best.

We sold my truck and paid Esther all the money back we had borrowed from her to buy the house.

Hurricane Alicia hit in August of 1983 and we stayed in our little green house. The house did not have any damage, just some of the fencing came down. We lost one phase of power; we could still use some electricity. Of course, we could not use our air conditioner. We could see on the transformer that one leg was disconnected. I went to work the next day and they put us on scouting for damages. Two people per vehicle and assigned an area for us. This was the easy part of the job. The hard part was drawing all the work orders.

We bought a new 1984 Buick LaSabre in November. We all took a trip, mom, DeAnn, Hugh, Jay, Joel, and myself. We went to the Smokey Mountains and to my brother Samuel's house for a couple of days. It rained extremely hard on the way home. We could not make the trip in one day due to the rain. We had to stop at a motel for the night.

In January of 1985, we took a trip to Winter Park, Colorado to do some snow skiing. Hugh, Jay, Joel, and I flew into Denver, Colorado. We rented a car and drove to Winter Park where we stayed in a condo. Our trip was short. We flew up on Friday and came back on Sunday. Even though the trip was short we all had a great time. The boys went through ski school the first day. After that we all skied together. I fell once and I could not see out of my glasses due to the ice. Three days go by really fast when you are having fun even when it is six degrees below zero.

We decided to add on to our house. A two story addition to the back along with knocking out the wall between the bedroom and the living room enlarging the living room. We also had a contractor install aluminum windows. We had a big undertaking going on. We were working on it every weekend. This project took awhile to complete along with hard work.

Along with the addition in 1985, we took a vacation to South Fork, Colorado to look at some land. The first land was nothing but desert, flat looking and we did not like it. Then we drove up into the mountains and found a place called Forbes Park. The land was being sold in three acre tracks. We took a tour of the area and absolutely fell in love with it. We signed all the papers to purchase the land. They told us that we could not stay on the land for two days. The elevation was a little over 10,000 feet above sea level. So, we went back into town with a Wal-Mart and bought all the camping gear we needed to stay on the land. One night we stayed at a place that had travel trailers. We fished for rainbow trout and the boys had a blast. The next morning we went on a horse back trail ride and we all had fun on this event. The next night we stayed at a National Forest Campground and cooked our fish on the coals of our campfire. Then we were able to go and camp on our land. There was not much to do. We just picked up limbs and stacked them. Hugh found a stream to fish in for awhile. It was very cold at night, the next morning we just slept in, we did not want to leave our warm sleeping bags. The next day we did the same thing along with walking around the block which was about one plus miles. The next day we had to head home. We awoke early since we had to leave and it was the 4th of July. I do not remember where we were on the way home but it was in the evening. I was driving about ninety miles per hour and in the distance we had the best view of a 4th of July fire works show. It was really beautiful.

I had Radial-Keratotomy eye surgery to correct my near sighted vision. It worked. No more glasses for me. Work then sent me to pole climbing school for two weeks in Lewisville. The first week was the book part. Then the second week we climbed telephone poles all day. The last day was test day. I passed. When I returned to Baytown, Hayes took me to the pole yard and made me climb a pole to check me out. When I got high enough he said "get down here".

We were bowling in a league, which mostly consisted of telephone people. Our team was Hugh, Mickey, Jamie Lyn, myself and Lonnie. Lonnie was coming back around and we did not care. He looked like he was having a hard time. I do not remember where we finished but we were towards the top.

In 1985 I was hospitalized three or four times at a mental hospital. The reason that I was hospitalized was because I could not sleep for four or five days and my body would crash, I could not think straight or anything. Even though my body crashed I still could not sleep. On one visit, Dr. Wren put me on another medication and after awhile I could not go to the restroom. So, he sent me to Dr. Fallon. After the examination, he said that I would have to catherize myself for the next two weeks each time I needed to use the restroom. I could not speak, surely he was wrong because a lot of the nurses can not even put in a catheter. But no as his nurse starts handing me everything I would need and explained what to do. That was the most miserable two weeks that I ever had. I wonder if he would have made a man do this.

Mania, a condition during which one's mood changes from normal to an extremely overactive state, is often marked by feelings of elation, expansiveness, or euphoria—a state often described as being "on top of the world." During a manic episode a person may sleep very little, talk very rapidly and continually, take little time to eat, show marked irritability and impatience, and have racing thoughts. Often the manic state progresses to the point where judgment is impaired and contact with reality is lost. It may become difficult to understand what a person is saying. Sometimes poorly thought-out decisions are acted on impulsively, with devastating financial, social, occupational, or legal consequences for self, family, and others. Hospitalization may be necessary for effective treatment. Mania and depression or recurrent manias alone are both called Bipolar I Disorder.

It is estimated that at least 13 out of every 1,000 people (1.3%) will have some form of manic-depressive illness during their lifetimes. But since depression can also occur in conditions other than manic-depressive disorder, it is estimated that as many as 150 out of every 1,000 people (15%) will experience at least one serious depression during their lives.

There is strong evidence from twin, family, and adoption studies that genetic or hereditary factors play a role in manic-depressive disorder. For example, close relatives of someone with the disorder are more likely to develop the disorder than the average person. Hereditary factors, however, are not apparent in the families of all persons with manic-depressive disorder and even when present, the specifics of genetic transmission are not well understood. As a result, it is not possible to predict accurately the risk for a given individual who has a relative with manic-depressive disorder.

There are different medications available to treat Bipolar Disorder and it can be controlled. Exercise and diet are very important. Most of the medications are monitored by a blood test every three months to check the level of the medication in your body. Whether it affects your liver, kidneys, thyroid or pancreas.

In 1986 we purchased a Prowler Lynx travel trailer. We needed a different vehicle to pull the trailer so we traded in our 1984 Buick for a 1986 Chevrolet van. We used the trailer all during hunting season. Hugh and two of his friends that he worked with at Upjohn found a deer lease in Center, Texas. I went out on one hunt and shot a five point white tail deer. Hugh killed a six and an eight pointer.

We took a trip to Winter Park, Colorado for a week during the Thanksgiving holiday. On this trip Hugh and I took Jay and Joel. We could not make it in one day so we stopped at a roadside park and slept in the van that night. The rest area was really nice. It had heated restrooms which was nice because the temperature was freezing. At Winter Park, there was not very much snow so we only stayed a couple of days. We then headed for South Fork, Colorado and stayed in a motel. There was plenty of snow there. We rented snowmobiles and rode those for a day. Jay rode with me and I was not a very good driver. I kept getting stuck in little creeks. Then we finally figure out the weight factor. They put Joel with me and I did not get stuck anymore. We all had fun anyway. We wanted to drive up the mountain pass towards Durango. It began to snow so hard you could barely see the road. I pulled over and turned around because we had already passed the sign that said to put snow chains on. We did not have any snow chains. We made it back down the mountain and to the motel. The boys played in the snow out in the parking lot and they were happy. Since we had done everything we could do, we headed home and had our Thanksgiving Dinner at home.

In February 1987 we went snow skiing. A whole group went with us this time. The group consisted of myself, Hugh, Jay, Joel, Lonnie and his girlfriend Jessa, and Lonnie's sister Lou. We flew up to Denver, Colorado on a Saturday morning and rented a car. We headed for Winter Park for our skiing. We all had a great deal of fun and hired a guy to video us skiing. When we saw this video it was also somewhat hilarious. While up there on this trip we found a delicious steak house. Time really flew by and it was time to go home. We left on a Monday.

Through our trips we realized that our luggage was not large enough. Immediately after returning from our skiing trip we headed to the mall to buy some larger luggage. We found what we wanted and went back home. Hungry, we dropped off the luggage at home and headed to the Monument Inn Restaurant for a seafood dinner. Everything was great as we had just come back from skiing and the memories were still at the front of our minds. The food was good. Nothing could disrupt our great time; or so we thought.

When we returned home from eating, Hugh noticed that something was wrong as soon as we pulled in our driveway. The bricks that he used to wedge in at the gate to keep it closed were knocked down. The latch on the driveway gate beside the house was unlatched. We went in the house and found it a mess. We had been robbed. The thieves had laid out all of our guns on the bed and took the old ones. They had stolen my 4–10 shotgun, 222 cal. rifle, Hugh's 20 gauge shot gun, and a 38 cal. pistol. Along with the guns they took a Kodak movie projector (which by the way was not working), a television, and some other stuff. To add insult to injury the thieves used our brand new luggage to haul off the stuff that they took. We called the sheriffs department and reported the robbery. They said that they would send a deputy out. After an hour without a deputy showing up we called again. After about twenty to thirty minutes we heard some noise upstairs. Hugh grabbed a gun and sat at the bottom of the stairs and I again called the sheriffs department and told them what was going on and that Hugh would shoot whoever he saw coming down the stairs. The deputy sheriff arrived within minutes, imagine that. The deputy did a search of the house and found no one. He took down all of the information. We had a record of the serial numbers of the guns stolen and the deputy took them. After all had somewhat settled down we found that the thieves had broken the window at the back of the house to gain entry. When we had returned home from eating we had interrupted them. They had run out the back yard dropping some items leaving a trail through the yard. But the trail soon ran out.

A week or two later, we received a call from the Harris County Sheriffs Department telling us that they had found our 38 cal. pistol and that they knew who pawned it. But to our amazement the district attorney would not file charges against this person, because of the elapsed time from the break in to the time the gun had been pawned. It was explained that he could have bought this gun. This is a bunch of hog wash. Even if he did not steal it (which I believe he did) I thought that it was against the law to have possession of stolen property! Thru a friend of ours we found that the name of the person who had pawned in our gun was Brian Scott Krieger. This character has a unibrow and lives in Lynchburg, which is close to our home. Hugh is still looking for him to this day. The last that Hugh has heard is that Krieger is in prison.

We really enjoyed snow skiing. I remember on two other occasions we took two of our nephews skiing for their graduation from high school. On one of the trips, a snow storm was coming in as we were trying to get home. We had to split-up and come home on two different planes. Our nephews thoroughly enjoyed these trips.

Over the 4th of July in 1987 we took two weeks off of work and headed for Forbes Park, Colorado. We hooked up the trailer and Hugh, Jay, Joel, mom, DeAnn, and two friends of the boys were on our way. We were weighted down pretty well. It was hard to make 55 mph without the trailer swaying. Although, the only part that I was worried about was the climb on the ranch itself. As it turned out the worrying was not in vain. During the climb we were going so slow that everyone but me jumped out of the van to lighten it and to push. I started picking up speed and I made it to the top of the hill. I sat and waited for everyone to get back in and off we went again. We had made arrangements with the guy that sold us the property to install a culvert so we could get the trailer on the land. When we arrived we found that the culvert was not where we could just pull on the land with a trailer. So we had to maneuver the trailer ever so slowly, then disconnect the van and adjust the position then reconnect. This went on for several hours. It was dark before we finally were able to get on the land and get set up. Throughout the two weeks we mowed grass and it sure looked good. It rained every afternoon. That was the time we sat around and did some beer drinking. The boys had fun riding their bicycles up and down the slopes. We never finished mowing the grass. After all there was three acres of sloping land and all we had was a push mower. We did go into town and bought another culvert. That was a sight. We had purchased a twenty foot culvert and tied it on the top of the van. It hung over the front and the back. The wind was blowing and it did not want to stay in place. Anyway we made it back to the land where Hugh installed it on the opposite side of our land. That sure made it easier when it was time to leave. Time sure went by fast. Before we knew it was time for us to be heading back home. It is always good to go on a vacation, but it is sure nice when you get back home.

In 1987 on a Saturday I made an emergency trip in to see Dr. Parik because I was hurting badly. He took me right in and said that I would have to have surgery. It ended up with me having to have a hysterectomy. I stayed in the hospital for several days. I remember waking up and hurting. When breakfast was brought in, I smelled the bacon and started throwing up. I asked them to take the bacon away and after the bacon was gone everything was okay. The only bad experience I had was I received a morphine shot and then got another one a little too close together. Dr. Parik told me I would never be hooked on drugs because I would not relax enough to let them work. I stayed off of work for six weeks recovering at home.

We had another deer lease in Concan, Texas, and we left the trailer on the lease. Hugh hunted every weekend and did not see anything. I did not hunt because I was still recovering from surgery. The night before the last hunt Hugh asked me to go with him and I said that I would. We were sitting there for about twenty minutes and I told Hugh that I saw a buck. He told me to shoot him. I told him that I could not get a good shot and for him to shoot. It was an eight point buck. In reality, I really could have shot the deer. It would not have felt right shooting the deer on my first trip out. Hugh had been hunting the whole season and had not seen a deer. I wanted him to take the shot.

On Thanksgiving we decided to rent a van and drive to Winter Park, Colorado. On the trip was Hugh, Jay, Joel, and their cousin Clifford, Esther, mom, DeAnn, and myself. It was windy and very cold on the drive there with snow flurries. We rented a condo for a couple of days and had our Thanksgiving Dinner. Esther took ski lessons. Mom and DeAnn stayed at the condo and the rest of us were on the mountain skiing. Esther decided skiing was not for her after taking lessons. We stayed a coupled of days skiing and then started heading back south. The tires on the van were getting very bare so we stopped in Walsenberg and bought four new tires. We decided since we were so close to our property in Forbes Park we would just drive there and see what it looks like covered with snow. It was beautiful. We got out and played around in the snow for awhile. It was getting late so we started heading for home.

In springtime, Hugh was coaching Little League Baseball. He had the Red Sox team. There was so much fundraising to do we were busy everyday. We had my mom baking for days making kolaches and cinnamon rolls. She baked hundreds of them and we never had any left over because they sold really fast. Jay and Joel played together the first year. The next year Jay did not want to play.

Hugh had been laid off again and we decided that he needed a different career path. We made the decision for him to enroll in a computer school for six months. When Hugh graduated from the computer school he was immediately hired by Chevron Information and Technologies. We sold that old truck of his and bought him a Geo Metro. The Geo's gas mileage was good and due to the distance that Hugh had to drive this saved us a lot of money.

For a couple of years Hugh and I played softball. Hugh would play with the GTE's men's team. Then if we could come up with enough players, I would play with the GTE's women team. We would play in different towns competing against other GTE teams.

I think this was around the time Hayes received a promotion which relocated him to San Angelo, Texas. The company brought in Phil to replace Hayes. Ollie was promoted to the 2nd line supervisor. Chase was over the other work group.

Here it goes again. Ollie moves me to a desk right to where he can watch me all day long. Of course, it is not long before I go to the hospital due to stress and not sleeping at night. After about three or four weeks of being in the hospital I went back to work and worked half days for awhile, then returned to full days.

We were always fishing during the spring for crappie (white perch) on DeAnn's property. We finally had to ask her to take over payments on the trailer because we could not afford it anymore. Gilbert and Monica, friends from work liked to go with us over the Easter holidays to go fishing. After Gilbert and Monica retired they moved back to their home town.

We are off for another two week vacation to our land in Forbes Park, Colorado. We went the last two weeks of June. All loaded up, Hugh, mom, DeAnn, Jay, Joel, three of our friends and of course myself and headed out. The traveling was slow because we were so weighted down. We enjoyed the scenery on the trip, going slower you can see more. When we arrived in Colorado our van starts missing out. We pulled over to a service station and parked behind it. We unhitched and rode into the next town and happened to find an auto parts man coming out of his store and he had the part we needed to fix the problem. We went to the trailer, fixed the problem and hitched it back up and off we went. We did not have far to go from where we broke down. Soon enough we were at the ranch gate. Here we go starting up the ranch road, we start getting slower and slower and when that needle hit six mile per hour, I yelled for everyone to bail out. They kind of hesitated and then doors started flying open and kids were jumping out. Hugh got out and even DeAnn was brave enough to jump from a moving vehicle. After everyone got out of the van, I started picking up speed and all was well. The kids thought that was great jumping from a moving vehicle. We arrived at our lot and set the trailer. We walked around the lot and drank some beer and the boys were off on their bikes as usual. Hugh headed for the stream to do some fishing while I cooked dinner.

The next day we headed into town that had a lumber yard. We wanted to build a picnic table. As it turned out they had redwood. When we returned back to our property Hugh was building the picnic table while I mowed the grass. One of our neighbors told us that after we leave and the new grass starts growing the deer are just all over our lot eating that tender grass. As usual the time goes by so fast and it is time to go home.

The summer of 1988 we made one more trip and this was our last one to our property in Colorado.

Hugh and a couple of his co-workers were going night fishing at the HL&P spillway one Friday night. It was around ten o'clock and Hugh went to check on the pistol to make sure it was loaded for me. Where we had added on to the house there was an uneven step between the old house and the new addition. Hugh somehow tripped walking thru that part and the pistol went off shooting himself in the ankle. One of his co-workers was already there and he and I were in the front yard talking. Hugh yells out, "Call 911 I shot myself." I ran into the living room and grabbed the phone and got 911 on the line. They wanted to know if he was shot with a shotgun, I said no. It was a pistol. Then they wanted to know if he was suicidal and I said no that he just tripped and the gun went off. Then the ambulance and sheriffs department arrived. The deputy sheriff asked the same questions, but when I showed him the uneven steps he could see how it could be accidental. I think half of Highlands were out in the street trying to see what was going on. The EMT's loaded Hugh in the ambulance and were ready to transport him to the hospital. The deputy sheriff was not thru with his investigation so Hugh's co-worker said he would stay until the sheriffs deputy was finished and he would lock up for me. So off we go to the hospital. The emergency room doctor just looks at it, wraps it up and we stay there about seven hours under observation. The doctor gave him a prescription for Tylenol 3 and tells Hugh to see an orthopedist. Now, Hugh still has a gunshot in his foot with bone fragments. We could not understand why the ER doctor did not call in an orthopedist right away. Hugh had to suffer with that foot from Friday night till Monday afternoon. The orthopedist even was upset that he was not called Friday night. The doctor scheduled him for surgery and Hugh was in San Jacinto Methodist Hospital for three days. They put him in the executive suite because of their inept emergency doctor.

In 1989 Joel woke us up late one night with his side hurting so we took him to the emergency room. The doctor immediately scheduled him for emergency appendectomy surgery. Joel had to stay in intensive care because of the drainage for two days and then another two days in a regular hospital room.

I had to have a discussion with Phil, my boss, about Barnard spreading all kinds of rumors about me. I told him that I hear them back through my family. He said that he would see what he could do.

6

We bought an eighteen foot Cajun center console bay boat at the boat show in Houston. The boat had a 140 hp Johnson motor. The boat was great and we went out in it every chance that we had. Of course it was not cheap to take out for a day. To fill the boat's gas tank up and gas for our vehicle to pull it, for bait, drinks, food, and whatnots we were spending one hundred dollars easy each trip.

I met with Dr. Wren every three months. On one of my visits Dr. Wren and I had a long talk. I was getting along so well that we decided to take me off of my medication.

After the first of the year in 1990, GTE said two people would have to work out of town. I was one of those that had to go and we worked in Port Lavaca for three months. Hugh and I drove down there and looked around because I had a choice of either receiving per diem of motel room and meals or so much cash money at a set rate each day. We found a trailer park on the Guadalupe River at a reasonable rate. We set a date to bring our travel trailer down. Barnard was the other worker going because the company goes by seniority and he has less than me. The trip down with the trailer went well and we set it up on a lot. Barnard stayed in a motel.

While on this three month assignment I had a company truck to drive. Now it was my first day of work in Port Lavaca, after finding the company building I was fine. I met Dan who was supervisor that I will be reporting to. I also met Derek and Oliver who were both techs. They all seemed so gracious and eager to get the help. I just fell right in and started working. Barnard showed up and he got acquainted. Within a week these guys had Barnard and I hooked on a breakfast taco, beans, hot sauce, and tea every morning. Barnard and I had not really gotten along very well because he liked to start rumors about me. Back at the trailer park a group of guys from out of state moved in and was working at a plant. After a couple of days, some of them came over and introduced themselves as Carson and Scott. They wanted to know what I was doing here by myself and I told them I was here on loan working and I hoped it would not be for very long. They told me well you come right on over and eat with us. We will take care of you. They were all nice and polite. Boy did they like to drink beer. Hugh and the boys would come to visit me on the weekends. After about two months had gone by, during spring break, I let Joel go home with one of them to Arkansas for a week. It looked like he had grown a foot when he came back.

We brought our boat and on the weekends we would fish out of Port O'Connor. We even rented a boat stall. We heard that you could catch a lot of shrimp so we bought a shrimp net. We tried shrimping, but we just could not find them. We caught a few just not many. One day bringing the boat in at the launch, Hugh let me off and I went and started backing the trailer up so we could load the boat. I had the trailer in line and when it was our turn I started backing it up. The only trouble was some gal was sitting there with her boat and would not move and her trailer was a couple of trailers back in line. I got out of the truck and sat on the tongue of the trailer. I looked up and there was a game warden at the marina. I hollered to him "Do you have any suggestions?" He said, "Yes, the gal with the boat needs to move out of the way so you can load your boat". The gal with the boat was not happy, but she did move.

Emery and Vada who owned the trailer park I was staying at had a forty-five foot shrimp boat. They asked us if we would like to go out with them shrimping. Hugh, myself, and Scott went with them. It was a great deal of fun. They knew just where to shrimp and every time we brought up the net it was full of shrimp. We put all the shrimp in the shrimp box and kicked the fish and crabs overboard. After the day was over they let us keep enough shrimp for everyone to have a meal.

I was standing on the river bank and I watched Joel and his friend go by in a boat and I saw Satan in between the boys. I hollered, "Stop Joel, come back." I jumped in the dirty muddy river to protect the boys. The river bank is straight up and down with just little roots coming out like a bunch of little twigs to hold on to. The river current was very swift. Joel gets to me pretty quickly and I tell the boys you are going to have to get me out of the river. So, I say to them 1–2–3 pull, but they were unable to get me out. The next time I told them you are going to have to give it all you have, now heave—ho, heave—ho, heave—ho and they had me out. Once they got me out of the water, I kind of lost it. One of the ladies came down to see if she could take me somewhere. I just touched her shoulder and all her buttons to her shirt started popping off, she turned and ran. The buttons popping off had to be the work of Satan. While running she turned and I said do not leave. I went in the trailer because I knew I was filthy from that water.

I got all of my clothes off and then someone was at the door. It was all the people at the trailer park. When they saw that I was naked they headed for their vehicles with me right behind them hollering wait, but they just kept going. I ran after them for awhile, but my mind was already racing and I just kept roaming around.

In a little while I heard sirens. It was an ambulance arrived. They came and threw blankets on me to get me down. I was pretty worked up by the time that they arrived. They put me in the ambulance and we headed to the Memorial Medical Center in Victoria. On the way I could not quit spitting. The tech asked me to quit and I could not even talk. He threw a wool blanket over my head and in a matter of minutes I had passed out.

The next thing I remember is someone asking why is she so dirty. Then I passed out again and when I awoke I found myself in a straight jacket in a secluded room. In a few minutes a tech comes in and asks how I was feeling? I told him okay except for the jacket. So, he takes the jacket off. I sat in that room for another hour or two. They then took me to another room which is in lock-up where they have the goofy mirrors. It was not very long before Hugh arrived. He gave me several baths to get me clean and he brought my clothes. He also left me Ollie's telephone number so I could call him in the morning. The next morning I was talking with a Dr. Spiller who said that the police were asking about a gun. I told him, "I have a pistol in the trailer and it is kept by the bed but the pistol was not out yesterday. They are welcome to check to see if it is in it's right place".

I made the call to Ollie. During the evening meal they served chicken fried steak and mashed potatoes with gravy. This little old man I was next to was shaking real bad and I could see he was having problems, so I just picked up his fork and knife and started cutting his steak in little pieces for him. You could just see the light come on in that man's eyes. No telling how long he had gone without eating. He started eating when I handed him his fork. When I got thru eating, the nurse at the counter wanted to know what made me do that. I told her it was just something that came to me in my head. She told me not to do it again that they would take care of it. One day Hugh came to visit me and I got a day pass so that we could get out and spend some time together. On the outing I bought a new pair of shoes. One of the patients wanted my old ones so I gave them to her.

Then it came time for me to be released. You really have to understand, a psychiatrist can get hung up on using a word. Dr. Spiller gave me a release to go back to work. In the release he used the word "judged". This terminology bothered me. Judged? I had not been taken to court nor had I been taken before a panel of psychiatrists. The term judge, to me was not appropriate. Upon my return to work I was reassigned back to Baytown. When I gave my supervisor Ollie my return to work paper from the doctor he immediately picked up on the word "judged" right away. He has been after me for awhile. This just gave him ammunition.

Ollie did not waste any time. He sent me to a doctor for the scabs on my arms. Ollie also made me sign a paper about my scabs to put in my file. Ollie never asks me about them. If he would have asked, I would have told him how I received them. They occurred when my dogs jump up on me every day causing scratches. Ollie once again started following me around out in the field. I found out that Ollie was not following anyone else. This behavior made me feel nervous and anxious. I again started the cycle of not sleeping. This continued for about three nights. Without sleep I find myself back in the hospital again. This time while in the hospital, I told a counselor that I did not think I could get any help here. He asked why? I said, "Because my boss was not following any of the other workers and for years he has stared at me all day long at my desk. I do not know what his intentions are and the other reason is that his wife is the secretary to the administrator of this hospital." He kind of fumbled his words and excused himself. I never saw him again. After my stay at the hospital, I was never admitted back to that hospital for mental health issues again.

The next time I needed to have medical attention for mental health issues I had to go to a different hospital. My insurance company found some kind of fifty mile rule and told me that I would have to go to Devereaux Hospital in League City. I was in the Devereaux Hospital for two or three weeks.

In July of 1991 we filed for bankruptcy. We just had more money going out than what was coming in. We had too much credit. We kept our house and the vehicle. We saved our money for two years so we could move into a new house. We had lived in our little green house for thirteen years.

After getting back home to our little green house one day, I was talking to Patti our next door neighbor. Patti told me that one evening, while sitting on her steps, from way up in the sky she saw a green fog coming down. The fog was making its way closer and closer to where she was. She did not know what was going on. It was eerie and then she saw that green fog go into my house. She was scared and went inside her house. Jay and Joel were at home and Hugh was working the evening shift. Joel thought that he heard something and got the neighbor next door to take a look but he did not find anything. I think this was God protecting my children.

7

After selling our little green house to our nephew Andrew and his wife. We bought a house in Highlands Trail Section II. There was only one hitch in this. It was that the sellers could stay in the house and rent it from us until their new house was finished.

We moved into my parent's house until we could get in our new home. This worked out good because their house was empty. My parents were living with DeAnn. It would not be long before we moved in our new house because the people whom we purchased it from were in a hurry to get their house. They were on the contractor to hurry all the time. While we were waiting to move to our new house, Hugh suggested that we go on a vacation. It sounded good to me. We headed to Indiana to visit some friends. We stayed there a couple of days then headed east northeast. Our adventure then took us to Pennsylvania, New York, and we ended up in Bar Harbor, Maine eating the best clam chowder and lobster. We stayed there a couple of days and headed home. On the way home we stopped at my brother Samuel's house to just say hi and then continued traveling. When we arrived home we found that we were still not able to move.

After being back from vacation for several days we received a phone call from the Liberty County Sheriffs Department. They asked if we had any guns stolen. Upon hearing this Hugh jumped up and started looking for the guns. We told them yes. We were missing several rifles and a shotgun. The sheriffs department told us that they have our guns and we would have to come and identify them to get them back. Hugh and I went to the sheriffs department to identify them and to our amazement they questioned us very harshly about the guns. Not that there was any question of the ownership of them, Hugh had his drivers license number engraved on all of them. After it was all over we found out that whoever stole them cut one of the shotgun barrels off too short. They were trying to find out if we did it. We were surprised to find out who stole the guns. One was a teenager that had been to our house many times.

Well, moving day finally did come and it was so nice to actually have a place to put everything. We bought a three bedroom brick house that had two baths and a large kitchen that overlooked the living room. It also had a dining room separated from the kitchen, a fireplace, a two car garage and in the back yard there was an in ground swimming pool. I absolutely loved the place. Shortly after we moved in, Hugh was really nervous about losing his job, so he transferred to Fourchon, Louisiana. Now we had to find him a place to live, somewhere near Fourchon. He first rented a place on Grand Isle for awhile, then moved to several other places. DeAnn bought a used motor home and let Hugh use it to live in. He parked it across the bayou from his work at a place call Charlie Hardisons. This time was difficult due to him not being at home with me. Although his schedule helped, he was working seven days on and seven days off.

All was not well in the sub-division. Some of the people there were a little strange and there were a lot of uneasiness between many of the neighbors. No one seemed to get along. Somebody must have let our three dogs out one night and they were barking. The next door neighbor calls me at 1:30 am and tells me that the dogs were barking and I just tell him it must be the Luna (moon). He did not like that answer because he hung up. I got up and let the dogs in. Oh, he also told me I should take them to have them trained not to bark. What a jerk, why would I want to have a dog that would not bark?

Joel had to have his tonsils removed because he was having so many sore throats. He stayed in the hospital a couple of days and this time he did not want me to stay with him.

Back to dogs, one time when Hugh was at home this same neighbor had his dog out in our front yard. Hugh was having words with him. I hollered out from the garage, I know how to get rid of his dog and I pointed an old broke B.B. gun at the dog. That did not even work.

Joel talked DeAnn into buying him a dirt bike. He was always riding it every Sunday on a dirt track with some of his friends. One Sunday, I went with him to the other side of Houston to a motocross track. Joel was racing and he ended up crashing his bike. An ambulance was called to take him to the hospital. He had broken a bone on the top of his foot. One of his friends brought his bike home for us. Joel had to see an orthopedist. There was not anything that could be done with the exception of keeping his foot wrapped and weight off of it. Have you ever tried keeping a teenager down? It was not easy. It was not two months later Joel and his cousin were out riding the dirt bikes and they ran into each other and Joel broke the same bone again. This time the orthopedist gave him a shoe to wear and told him to stay on the crutches. As soon as we got home, Joel said "I am not going to wear this shoe".

We were still having trouble with several of the neighbors, and one of the neighbors took us and another neighbor to court. I cannot even remember why now. When we get to court the judge looks straight at me and asks what's going on. I told him when we moved in the neighborhood we all got along fine. We had gone to dinner at one of the complainant's houses and there really is just no reason why we should not be getting along. Everyone should just mind their own business. The judge just repeated what I said and dismissed the case. I can not remember the name of the neighbor, but his brother-in-law was a lawyer. I told the brother-in-law that I knew there was something wrong with my neighbor and they better keep him away from my family.

At this time in our lives we decided to hire a realtor to help us find a buyer for our house and to help us find a contractor to build a new house. With all the problems that we were having with our neighbors this was the only thing that we could do to give us peace of mind. That place was the neighborhood from hell. When we had left the neighborhood, I left saying that I wish that I could win the lottery and give the house to the lowest scum in Highlands.

My nephew moved out of the green house. The San Jacinto River had flooded around this time. We let a family rent the brick house but all they did was tear it up and not pay the rent. We finally sold the green house to the Townley's. They lived down in the river bottoms by Hugh's Granny. We had moved into an apartment in Baytown. We were having a hard time finding a lot that we liked within the location we wanted. We were still not happy with the lot that we had picked.

Hugh and I went out to the Hill Country one weekend just to get out of town. We stopped at a convenience store and Hugh began talking to a guy, the next thing you know we are off looking at some land. The land was very impressive. It had a big draw, water, electricity and easy access. We only had one problem; the deal with our realtor at home. An architect had already drawn up the blue prints for the new house. I got elected to call and I told him that we were going to have to back out of our deal and that I was sorry. I still intend to make things right on that deal.

Well as it come to pass we did not win the lottery, but some other family that lived in the older section of town did. I found it quite delightful that they ended up buying our house in Highlands Trail II. Justice was served.

So we bought 86 acres in Eagle Ridge Ranch. The closest town was Rock-springs. The white tail deer were plentiful. Axis deer and turkeys also ran wild. We put out game feeders and deer blinds.

One weekend when Hugh came home from Louisiana he stopped by to see one of his friends and had a few drinks. Okay, maybe more than a few drinks. When I got home from work Hugh had dinner ready for me. I told him I was not hungry right then and that I would eat later. He got very upset and locked himself in the bathroom and would not come out.

We had to call his friend to get him out of the bathroom. Meanwhile, I was talking to April and she was finding a facility that we could take him to in the morning. In the morning, I told him there was a place I thought he should go see and talk with them about his problem with excessive drinking. He agreed. The place was in Kingwood and he stayed there on a program for thirty days. When he came out, you could see the difference in him. His personality has changed and it was nice to be able to be around him again. It was hunting season so we headed for Rocksprings. Hugh got an 8 point buck and won the Big Buck Contest the landowners were having. During this trip we began to build a cabin. Before leaving we had framed it up and thought we had braced it good enough. Then we left and headed back home.

A short time after we came back Hugh's dad Cory passed away. Hugh did not want to go for the graveside service. He was pretty upset so we took a few days off and headed back to Rocksprings. Just as we were passing through Rocksprings heading for the ranch Hugh was pulled over and he received a driving award (speeding ticket). About twenty minutes later we arrived at the ranch where we found that our bracing to the cabin was not good enough. The cabin frame had blown down. This just was not our day. We were taking two weeks vacation to build the cabin so we moved the location and started from scratch. It was in February and it was cold. We were sleeping in a tent and had a campfire for heat. With Hugh, Jay, Joel, DeAnn and myself helping to build the cabin, we got it built and dried-in. Every time we went back we worked on the cabin for the whole weekend. We even had the entire property fenced. We bought an old building from the owner of the Lumber, Hardware and Feed Store in town and placed it to the rear of our cabin. Then the owner of the feed store gave us two Angus bull calves and nine heifer calves so we could apply for the AG exemption on our property. A couple of years later we had a septic tank installed.

8

Fantastic news at work, there was a job bid opening in a town called Floresville, which is about 30 miles east of San Antonio. Better yet, the boss's name on the bid is one of them that I had met in Port Lavaca. He was from Robstown. I got all my paper work in and faxed the bid in right away. Steve calls me from Robstown and asks if I really want the job and I said, "I really do." He told me they were excited about having me in the position. Goody-Goody gum-drops I was leaving Baytown! In about two days some yo-yo calls me and says his name is Wylie from Dickinson and wants me to let him have the Floresville job. I told him no. He just kept on whining. I just told him I have been waiting to get out of Baytown for a long time so no.

Hugh and I made a trip to Floresville to look the town over and find a place for me to live. We found the office and met a couple of the installers. That night we stayed in a motel and found a rent house in the newspaper in a town called Poth. We called and made an appointment with the guy to look at it and he said come on over he was there. It was an older three bedroom house with hardwood floors that I love. The price was what we could afford to pay and it was only six miles east of Floresville. The backyard was fenced so I could let the dogs out when I got home.

When we arrived back to Baytown I called a moving company to make the arrangements to move our belongings. They were going to pack everything in the apartment then go to my office and get my desk, chair, mark system, and table, then go to our storage building and pack everything there. On moving day they did not waste any time. They went to all three places, loaded everything and were ready to head out the next morning. I met Steve and Toby the next afternoon.

When we arrived in Poth the movers unloaded my office things. Steve and Toby were loading the office equipment into a company truck and took it to the office in Floresville for me. Toby was my boss. They told me I did not have to be to work until in the morning. So, DeAnn and I went to work and started unpacking. While there I ran my phone line. When morning came I went to work and Toby was there, but I am going to stop here, I want to say that I have never met a finer group of men than those who worked in the Floresville office. They are true gentlemen and have my highest regards. Of course, Floresville had a good Mexican Food Restaurant. I would eat breakfast tacos every morning with hot sauce.

We got a call from Joel who said that Bryanne was in the hospital having the baby. We made arrangements to take off from work and drive to Baytown for the arrival of our first granddaughter. They named her Summer and she was born in June of 1996.

Some time later, Hugh and I were at the ranch in Rocksprings like we normally were on most weekends. We spent our time feeding our cattle and deer and working to finish the cabin. When it was time to load the vehicle and head home some rain clouds came up. I was in the cabin handing everything to Hugh as he was standing at the tailgate when all of a sudden bam, a lightning bolt hit about five feet from Hugh. We had an Isuzu Rodeo and Hugh quickly jumped in the front seat. We hurriedly finished packing and were on our way. We had made it to the first gate when Joel called and told us that my dad had passed away. I think that the lightening bolt was a sign from God telling me that my dad had passed.

The time flew by. Joel and Bryanne decided to get married in October of 1996 and there was so much to do. We were living in Poth and we had to go to Baytown and cook the rehearsal dinner. After the wedding, Joel and Bryanne left for their honeymoon. Hugh and I stayed in a local motel and kept Summer with us until the newlyweds returned.

I was working 4–10's with Fridays off. This offered me a lot of time to be at the ranch. DeAnn would come down on Thursdays and we would head to the ranch when I got off of work. Hugh was still working in Louisiana and came to the ranch when he was off. While at the ranch I enjoyed putting a pot of beans on to cook and sitting under the shade tree drinking beer. I did not drink a whole lot, just sipping on a beer while cooking beans. Then when it was time, I would grill the meat.

Life was so good and then I got the rug pulled out from underneath me. They transferred Wylie to our jobsite. My worst nightmare rode into town. He was okay at the beginning. From now on though, the central office techs Nate and Hape had to take breaks with him alone instead of all of us together. Chad, who was the manager over the contractors, had to use my truck one time and he fixed the air conditioning. My son Joel could not find a job around Baytown so I told him to come here and I would get him a job. I got him a job with Henckels &

McCoy. DeAnn helped Joel out getting a double-wide trailer on seven acres of land.

I took money out of my savings to fence Joel's property and to put in a driveway. Hugh was going to rent a place to live in Louisiana with a guy from work. I decided to move into the motor home on Joel's property. This was good because the house that I was living in was a drafty old house. On one occasion I had come home and all of the jets to the gas stove were open full blast. I got the dogs out and shut the stove off. Fortunately because of the draft in the house, nothing serious happened. The stove was very old and did not work properly.

Everything was going along fine until one Friday night when Hugh, Joel and I were out late digging fence post holes and then setting the fence post. We were all tired and I would even challenge Joel by telling him that I would give him $100 for just one more. Bryanne was not happy about us staying out so late and she got upset. She got so upset that a couple of days later all my furniture that they had borrowed was thrown out the front door. I wondered what was going on, so I told DeAnn to get the truck keys from him. DeAnn was paying for the truck. I happened to walk behind the mobile home because I was putting all my items underneath the trailer and Bryanne was cussing like a sailor. The next morning Joel and Bryanne rented a U-Haul, packed up and left. We caught all the utility people just in time because they were having the utilities shut off. My granddaughter Summer had some pictures made at Wal-Mart in Seguin and since I paid for them I wanted them. DeAnn and I went to Wal-Mart and got the pictures. They just up and ran away because Joel was working on his property a little late. We put the land up for sale. I found an apartment in Seguin to rent and we moved the motor home to our property in Rocksprings.

Back at work, Wylie was trying his hardest to get rid of me and I do not know why. One of the installers named Winston showed me where Wylie would go back in the central office and listen in on my phone calls. I listened in on one of Wylie's calls when he was talking to a technician in Robstown. According to the conversation, Wylie had a plan to do something to me and the tech in Robstown told him that he had better be very careful.

One Thursday, I cooked a big one pot meal for all the guys and they liked it. There were leftovers and Hape said he would take them. When I got back to work Monday my pot was no where to be found. I was able to get in touch with Hape and he said he put it on the table. Come to find out, the cleaning people had found it in the trash. Now imagine that!

One day Toby came thru asking if I needed any clips for my test set and I told him no I had a couple pair. Well, I got curious after he left. I went to my truck, unlocked the tool box and grabbed my tool bag. When I opened the tool bag I found that it was half full of clips. My tool bag can hold climbing gear. I wonder where Wylie got all those clips from. I guess he thought that I would walk out and show Toby my clips or something. A couple of days later, when I was out in the field, I decided to check the bag again. Wylie had taken every clip out of it. I was working a lot of hours now and had been for awhile. I was working fourteen to fifteen hours a day. Sometimes I would have to go to Robstown to where the boss was located. Lottie is the secretary and we would always go to lunch together.

Joel leaving like he did upset me and the long hours at work were getting to me. I had been working fourteen to fifteen hours a day for a long time. Hugh had been home on one of his seven days off and it was time for him to leave, I asked him not to go because I did not want to be alone. He said that he had to go to work. I knew something was going to happen to me. It was just a feeling. Just as soon as he left I thought I would take a bath. I made the bath water way too hot. Then I put some lotion on and I got lotion everywhere, I slipped and fell. I laid on the bathroom floor for awhile and my mind was racing and going into a high. I did not have any clothes on because I was going to take a bath. The next thing I knew I found myself on the living room floor. I was in and out of being conscious and I heard a person who kept wanting me to repeat what he was saying. When he got to one part I refused and, in a very loud voice he said "I thought you said that she was ready" A voice then said, "You know what to do." All of a sudden I was brought upright to my feet and then in my mind started spinning very rapidly. I sure hope I was not stepping on any of those snakes that were around me. The next thing I knew, the sliding glass doors opened and out they push me. I just stood there dumbfounded. Satan had really gotten to me this time. I still stood my ground and it made him mad. My mind was all in confusion and I had hit a high on my bipolar. It was cold outside and I just headed for the lights. I hid in some hedges and after awhile I heard sirens. The man at the convenience store recognized me. He called his wife who is the manager of the apartments where we were living. She contacted Hugh. Meanwhile, the police were trying to calm me down, I was showing them how high I could jump. Finally, they get me to calm down and handcuffed me and put me in a patrol car. They took me to the Seguin Hospital Emergency Room. I was talking up a storm. When I am on a high with my bipolar my mouth gets into high gear. Hugh told them who my doctor was and they contacted him. It took my doctor a long time to get there. I was laying down and I heard someone loudly say take her to state. Then once again take her to state. My doctor, Dr. Quitman, was telling them to take me to the State Hospital. He did not even come over to me and ask me any questions to evaluate my mental state of mind. I had insurance. I can go to a private hospital. People that do not have insurance go to state. What kind of a doctor was he?

The social worker at the hospital found a psychiatrist named Dr. Benson at Laurel Ridge that would treat me. The social worker also said that she would testify in our behalf if we decide to sue Dr. Quitman. And she said we really did need to sue him. The Seguin Police Department drove me to Laurel Ridge. Dr. Benson's practice is Christian based. I told Dr. Benson that I was Jesus when I was admitted. I was in a blackout and did not remember saying this to him. I later found this out when I wrote and asked for my file. When I came to my senses, I knew that I was not Jesus.

I liked the therapy groups and the outdoor activities were awesome at the Laurel Ridge Hospital. I especially liked Dr. Benson. I guess I should have told him exactly what had happened to me, but I thought it would be best, just to keep my mouth shut. I stayed at Laurel Ridge Hospital somewhere around three or four weeks. I felt a lot better when I left.

When I returned back to work, I eased into it slowly. That did not last long because everything was backed up and I had to pick up the pace back to full blast. This is fine with me because I am not sick anymore.

Two weeks later I went to Baytown to visit my granddaughter Summer at Joel's apartment. I got there Thursday night and Friday morning I was feeling very bad in my chest. I asked Joel to take me to the hospital. He said, "don't you just need a doctor?" I told him no and to get me to the emergency room. He did and they took me back right away and x-rayed me. I had pneumonia and they admitted me to the hospital. I was not getting better. I kept blowing out the IV that was in my arm and nobody in the hospital could put an IV in me. Then the insurance had a problem with me being in the hospital so many days. They moved me to the old hospital on Decker Drive. I stayed there a couple of days. After I was there a few days they decided to move me back to the first hospital, but before they could, they needed to draw a blood sample. The only way they could get it was out of my finger tips. After I was moved back to the first hospital a decision was made to move me to Methodist Hospital downtown Houston so that I could see a Pulmonary Specialist. I guess that when the windstorm blew in with all the red dust, the dust irritated me causing the pneumonia.

The specialist wanted to do a procedure to scrape my lungs to get a culture to find out what kind of pneumonia I had. The only problem was that I had to be awake while he did the procedure. Normally they put you to sleep. He started by running a tube up my nose with liquid and it was uncomfortable. Fortunately it was all over pretty quick. I stayed in the hospital a total of ten days.

After I was released from the hospital, I had to stay at Joel's apartment because I was on oxygen constantly and very weak. The first morning that I was there Joel went to work. I got hungry, so I got up and made me something to eat. Bryanne and Summer did not come out. I stayed a couple of days at Joel's apartment. As soon as I was able to get off of the oxygen, Hugh took me home to Seguin. I had the old-fashioned pneumonia that people got years ago. I kept bronchitis for awhile. This sickness really knocked me down. When I went back to work and they had hired another technician. We had enough work because the Floresville area was growing rapidly.

9

Hugh called me one morning and said that there was a job opening in Mont Belvieu and that he was going to put in for it. Mont Belvieu is close to Baytown. He wanted me to come back home too. Oh, how I did not want to go, but I called Toby and he said there was a tech opening in Dickinson. Dickinson is not far from Baytown. Toby tried to talk me out of it and even asked me to remember how they are down there. I know, I did not want to go, but I had to. I filled the paperwork out and faxed it in and in a couple of days human resources called and offered me the position. They wanted to know the answer right then and I said yes. I called a moving company and made arrangements for them to pack all my belongings at the apartment to take them to Baytown where we had rented an apartment. On my last day at work in Floresville, Toby, the installers and the new tech gave me a going away party after work outside the cantina next door to the office. They grilled steaks and baked potatoes and we drank beer and really had a great time.

I did not talk to any of the bosses in Dickinson before I moved. We moved into an apartment on a Wednesday and I went to work the next morning. My new bosses name was Will. Will wanted to know why I had not come to work yesterday afternoon. I told him because we were moving and I did not know I was supposed to report in for work. He said that he did not know how he was supposed to show the four hours. I told him that I would come in the next day, which was my normal day off, and make up the hours. He seemed to be relieved and said okay. The office was horrible. You only had a tiny little space to sit in but I became use to it and everything was okay for awhile.

The clerk Lulu was a little strange. She talked very sharply, almost to the point of being rude. I would get there early in the morning, make coffee and one of the engineers named Charlie and I would drink a cup of coffee out back. Will left me in charge a couple of times when he was on vacation. He gave me these large road move jobs to work on and I had never worked on a road move job before, not even in Baytown. Most of my work in Floresville was facility work. So I was really put in a very bad position.

Charlie, his wife Dara and I were driving to our ranch in Rocksprings one Friday morning in November. They were in their car and I was in my truck. We were on Interstate 10 right around Luling when my right front tire just lost all the air. I sure was glad Charlie was with me to help change that tire. When we got to the ranch Joel called and said that my mom had passed away. She just stopped breathing. I think God was telling me once again by the flat tire that my Mom had passed on.

In February 1998, my second granddaughter was born. The whole family was there to welcome her in to this world. As soon as we saw her we all fell in love. She was named Josey. I took a two week vacation after she was born to help Joel and Bryanne get settled in with the new little one.

10

We moved to Webster and rented a two bedroom apartment and Jay moved in with us. One night when I laid down in bed and I heard my name very, very loudly coming from a bullhorn like it was in heaven echoing Diane Cornelius. I did not know what that meant but I did not sleep for a couple of nights. Due to the lack of sleep I had to go to the hospital. I stayed there for a couple of weeks.

We helped Jay buy a vehicle. Jay never asked us for much help after he moved out on his own, just this one vehicle. He moved back in so he could save some money. I rarely saw him except on the weekends. On the weekends we would go grocery shopping together. Hugh, Jay and I went on a four day trip to Las Vegas. We flew out of Hobby Airport early one morning and we stayed at the MGM Grand. Jay and I just played the slots and Hugh played black-jack. We walked around looking at all the hotels and also spent some time touring the Hoover Dam. Time flew by and we were back at the airport on our way home and did not win any money. Although we had not won any money, we did not really loose much either.

I went back to work and they had brought in some new furniture. Everyone now had their own cubicle with a lot more space and the office looked a lot nicer. I was starting to have trouble concentrating on my work. I felt stress coming on due to the fact that I had not been fully trained for the work that I was being assigned.

11

We wanted to move back to Baytown. Although the apartments that we had rented were okay, we really wanted to buy our own place. In 2000 we purchased a mobile home and moved it to a mobile home community in Baytown. When we moved to Baytown Jay moved back out on his own. What bothers me now is that I have not talked to him nor seen him since he moved back out. He just moved right on out of our lives. I keep praying that one day he will knock on my door and say "Hi Mom".

In March 2000 I helped Joel attain a job with Verizon in an outside position. He tried to transfer to a splicing job in Baytown as soon as he could. When a splicing job came open Joel took the test. Joel's supervisor Floyd told him he did not pass the test. Floyd gave the job to one of his other workers. When another splicing job came open, Joel put in for this one also. Human resources said he could have the job. Joel asked about the test and the representative from human resources said that he had passed the test. So, Floyd lied to Joel just because he wanted to put another guy in that splicing job. What a low life to tell somebody they failed a test. Floyd should had just told Joel the truth.

We decided to sell the ranch in Rocksprings because of the six hour drive it takes from living in Baytown. I really missed going every weekend and having my granddaughter Summer with me. She loved feeding the cows. She would get a handful of hay and walk up to them and try to get them to eat it. The ranch was not on the market long before it sold. As it turned out it was a blessing that we did sell the ranch.

In May 2000 our family grew again. Our grandson was born in May and they named him Jude. We were at the hospital when he was born. All the family was there and everyone held him. He received a lot of loving his first few hours of life. Now we have two granddaughters and a grandson. We had helped Joel and Bryanne get into a house they had found. We put the down payment and had the house financed in our name. Joel eventually paid us back the down payment.

Joel talks me into helping him buy a truck. We made the deal with a Ford dealership and off he goes home with a brand new 2001 Ford F150 truck. There is something wrong with it, so he took it back for service. I do not exactly remember how many times he takes it back, but they give him a loaner truck. Joel and a couple of his friends went out drinking one night and took the loaner truck and run it thru a vacant field after it had rained. When he took the loaner truck back, I got a call and the dealership wanted to know what had happened to the truck. I did not know anything because Joel had not told me a thing. The front grille was broke. I called Joel to ask what happened. He told me that they drove the truck thru a field, hit a bird and got stuck. The Ford place told me there was grass and mud in the transmission case and my insurance was not going to pay. I had to pay $450 out of my own pocket to fix the loaner truck. Next, Joel claimed that they still had not fixed his truck so he backed out of buying the truck. This left me having to deal with the Ford place because I had signed a contract. I basically swapped it for a 2001 Crown Victoria.

I separated from Hugh and got my own apartment. I guess I was gone about a month and he talks me into coming back to him.

My supervisor Will put in for retirement. I applied for his supervisor position but, it really did not matter to me if I got his position or not because of the responsibility and my illness. I just put in for it to see what the company would do. They interviewed me and re-interviewed me a couple more times. They hired an ex-employee off the street named Elmer. Elmer came in there with a chip on his shoulder. He said show me that tech gal that wanted to be boss. She will not work for me. In the meantime, Dr. Wren was advising me to take a medical retirement. I put in for one and went out on medical leave. I stayed out on medical leave for nine months. Verizon contacted my doctor and told him to just give me more medication and send me back to work. I had to go back to work because I had no more sick time left. On my first day back to work they sent me back home for disciplinary reasons. Then I had the rest of the year off because of vacations.

When I got back to work after the first of the year and start working. Elmer thought that I did not know anything. He also thought the same about his boss Potsie because they wanted to give me these little bitty jobs. Elmer wanted to control them. I had to ask him in the morning how many splicing hours to put on a job. Then before I input it in the computer I had to ask him again about the splicing hours and he always ranted and raved. He would say that they were wrong, even though it was him who decided the numbers of hours. He came in smelling of liquor, cologne and cigarettes in the morning.

While I was out in the field one day verifying the counts in an X-Connect Box I heard a voice. It was telling me, do not fly, do not fly. It happened for a couple of days but I had no idea what it meant and I was not going on a trip anywhere. This happened about four months before 9–11.

12

We bought two acres in a mobile home subdivision in Dayton in June 2001. The lot was nothing but trees and brush. Hugh rented a bull-dozer and he and Joel cleared the lot leaving some trees. We had the trailer moved and set up in one day. The air conditioning man was there to hook-up our air conditioner and Hugh wired the electricity to the trailer. We had not been there two weeks when a tropical storm hit and the water was real high on our land. Hugh had to go outside and block up the air conditioner condenser.

Back at work whenever I would input a job in the computer and release for approval the computer would approve the jobs and send it direct to Charlie, by passing Elmer. I was to the point to where I did not want to play silly little games that they were playing. I knew what they were doing. I just kept my mouth shut and did my work.

I was unhappy with Hugh and in confusion and decided to move out and get my own apartment in Baytown in January 2002. My mind was confused most of the time and I just wanted to be alone. It was not long before I became sick. I called Joel and asked him to go to the store and get some soup for me to last thru the weekend because I was not able to get out myself. He said that he would but he never did bring me anything or call me all weekend. I did not eat anything all weekend and could not sleep. I got sick and I could not get in to see the doctor on the day that I called in. My son Joel took me to the emergency room on Monday night, February 25, 2002. I saw Dr. Wren and they had to release me due to my insurance. The next day Joel took me to Devereaux in League City. I was released on March 4, 2002. When I was released Hugh moved me back to Dayton.

When I go back to work, I thought everything was fine, but around 4:30 in the afternoon I got called into Potsie's office with Elmer and Lulu and union representative. Elmer read me a letter that stated that one of my days off was unexcused and Verizon was terminating my employment. I told him that it was probably just an error. I offered to call my doctor to get it straightened out. Elmer escorted me to my desk where I got all my personal items. He followed me to my car and told me that I could beat this.

We had a meeting a couple of days later and I produced a letter from my doctor clearing the February 25, 2002 date. Potsie and Lulu were shooting daggers big-time. The third-line supervisor was conferenced in on the phone. He asked me if I wanted my job back or wanted to try for a medical retirement. I told him I wanted to try for a medical retirement. Then later on the grievance that I had filed with the company was disregarded by the company. They indicated that it was not a grievance. The union called and asked if I wanted my job back and I told them no that this would just happen again. We had a lawyer look at suing Verizon. The lawyer Leo got a package of medical records about me. He called me all nervous and said that they must have been watching me and heard that I wanted to quit taking my medication. I gave him a song and a dance because the guy thought that he was looking at Verizon's insurance company's paperwork. All he was looking at is what I had authorized my doctor to release from his files to give to Verizon. I quickly got rid of Leo. He did not even know what he was looking at and was getting highly agitated because he did not want this case. I definitely did not want his representation.

Over in Baytown, they could not find anything for Barnard to do except gossip, start rumors and sing nasty songs so they promote him. He still could not do his job and Charlie from Dickinson had to come and do it for him. When a female second line supervisor over them figured out what was going on Barnard had to learn how to do his own job. She also canned Elmer. Back in Floresville, Wylie was promoted to the management job. Everybody either retired, transferred or quit, including installers. Talk about cleaning house. So much for him. When Verizon terminated me I had twenty three years, four months service. I can apply for my pension at age 55. Even after all that happened, Verizon is a good company to work for, it's just some ignorant people work for them.

I applied for unemployment and social security disability. The unemployment came in pretty quick. I had to go to their office and get on a computer and search for jobs. After awhile I had to call in every so often and could stay at home and search for jobs. Social Security called and interviewed me over the phone and sent a lot of paperwork. I got it all filled out and returned to them.

I was having some medical problems with my stomach. I could not eat red meat. My doctor gave me a pill to settle my stomach down. I was walking an hour every morning. I spent a great deal of time at the doctor's office in 2002 due to various illnesses.

Then a check from social security came in the mail. They had approved me for Social Security Disability. Hugh had checked the mail and came in and told me that my first social security check had come in, but we could not cash it, that they had made a mistake. The amount was substantial. We called the social security office and they said that it was correct. They went back to the time that I had been off of work and reimbursed to that time. This really helped us out with all the bills that had been piling up.

Hugh wanted to take a vacation and ride the motorcycle to South Dakota. I kept telling him no. I thought about it and since I was used to the heat I told him I would go. We had a motorcycle trailer that we pulled with the motorcycle. Inside it I had cooking utensils, Coleman stove, food, clothes, tent, cot, chairs and sleeping bags. On the tongue of the trailer was an ice chest. We left Dayton the first week of August 2002 and it was very hot. We stayed in a motel the first night because we stopped early it was so hot. The next day we made it to Raton, New Mexico and stayed at the KOA Campground. I would get up and walk an hour every morning before making breakfast. We made it to South Dakota and stayed at the KOA in Deadwood. We went to Sturgis because Hugh wanted to find him a good leather jacket and he did. We were there a week before the rally started. We then went to Mt. Rushmore and rode in the Blackhills.

We left and headed for South Fork, Colorado. We camped in the National Forest and fished for rainbow trout which we ate nearly every meal. One day we made a ride to Durango, Silverton, and Ouray then back to South Fork. It was a very beautiful ride on a motorcycle and it took all day. When we got back it was after dark.

There was a bear that got into the garbage can one night. The manager of the campground let us use his shotgun just in case the bear came back. We were the only ones in the campground. The bear never came back. The last night there we stayed in a motel then left for home. I had a really good time and would like to go on another motorcycle trip if my back will allow it.

When we got back home I had a letter from Verizon in the mail. They denied the medical retirement. I kind of knew they were going to deny it.

My mind was still all confused. I would get up and walk an hour every morning. A voice told me to stop taking my pill. That voice told me that for about three days. Then about six months later, I became exhausted around noon time. I had increased my walking to the afternoon also. I went to Dr. Wren and told him what was going on. He sent me to have my blood checked. My blood work was okay. I still complained to him that something was wrong. He told me that there was another test-a 24 hour clearance test that we could do. I did that test and it came back positive, I was having kidney failure. Dr. Wren told me to go to a renal specialist. I could not get in to see anyone in Baytown for a month, so I went to the Diagnostic Clinic in Houston. I saw a Dr. Holley and he determined that my kidney failure was due to the Lithium medication that I was taking. He called Dr. Wren and advised him that I would have to get off of Lithium. As it turned out I had sixty percent kidney failure. Dr. Wren and I discussed what medication to put me on. I elected to take Depakote ER because I think Dr. Wren had tried the other choice I had and I was allergic to it. I could continue my hour walk in the morning, but that was all the activity I could do.

I was in the car going with Bryanne somewhere and the subject of me not feeling good came up and she said, "Oh, you just want to be sick". I was just too weak to argue and could not believe she would say that.

With my mind still all in confusion and weak it came to me on November 20, 2003. I went to the mall to a Christian Bookstore and bought a Bible. When I got home I started reading the Bible. I was reading it every chance I got; I could not put it down. Hugh even commented asking me if I remembered where I left off every time that I would pick it back up. Somewhere along while I was reading, Jesus came into my heart and all the confusion and voices in my mind just went away. It felt wonderful. Jesus was in my heart and my mind was free. I had rededicated my life to Jesus and my Lord and Savior. It did not take me long to finish reading the entire Bible. My kidneys are functioning normal for my age now.

Next, I was on Hugh to take me to church. It took a long time to convince him that I really wanted to go. He finally agreed and we went to a couple of churches. We decided to try the church along the highway in front of our subdivision. It was called Woodland Hills Chapel. It was okay, so that is where we started going. I was baptized August 1, 2004 at Rural Shade Baptist Church. The church was in trailers and a church building became vacant so a vote was taken to move to the church building. I bought Hugh a Bible for his birthday. I served on a couple of committees and made some good friends at Woodland Hills Baptist Church.

We stayed at Woodland Hills Baptist Church for three years then we became aggravated at all the fussing and fighting going on all the time. We started going to different churches. Then Peg and Hank asked us to come and visit their church. They said that they had a real good preacher. We picked them up one Sunday and they were right. He was a good preacher. We joined Tabernacle Baptist Church shortly thereafter.

We had been on several fishing trips over the years with Captain Joe in Corpus Christi. He would take us to Lower Laguna Madre and Baffin Bay. We took the grandkids a couple of years. We usually limited out on speckled trout. In 2006 I caught a 27" speckled trout. I had never caught one that big before.

Before we knew it, Hurricane Rita was headed our way. Hugh and I already had motel reservations in Ozona to look at some land in west Texas. This was a blessing to have a place to go, the whole south east Texas area was evacuating. We got caught in all the evacuation from the hurricane. It took us thirty hours to get to Ozona, normally a nine hour trip. We looked at the land and we liked it. Another couple went in with us to buy it. So we bought 200 acres with the nearest town being Dryden. We hung around Ozona a couple of days before heading home. When we get back home, we had no electricity or water. We had to stay at Joel's. Then, my brother-in-law Lawrence calls and says somebody needed to come get DeAnn. She was not doing well, there was no electricity or water and he thought that she has dementia. The next morning Summer, Jude and I make a trip to Lake Sam Rayburn to get her. She did not want to go at first but we talk her into it. She had a Pomeranian dog and I had one too and I knew that was not going to work out with Bryanne. Everything was going along fine until Bryanne's mother came over strolling through the house with her female dog. DeAnn's male dog got excited and peed on the corner of the furniture. Bryanne made a big deal of it and said that they could not afford to buy new furniture. She said the dogs would have to go outside. These dogs were thirteen years old and had never slept outside in their life. The heat would have killed them. In the meantime, Hugh had bought a generator and he was outside with it. I told him what happened and he said let's go home. Bryanne could not even give us a place to stay after everything Hugh and I had done for them throughout the years and are still doing to this day.

We went back to DeAnn's and met with a realtor and put her place up for sale. While we were there DeAnn fell and broke her wrist so we had to take her to the hospital. When we got her back home, the orthopedist did surgery on her wrist. Joel and I were going up on weekends and cleaning and going thru everything in her trailer. It was a major task. It took us two months to completely empty the trailer and clean it. I even had help from my friend Stacy a couple of times.

I had to take DeAnn to a neurologist to confirm that she had dementia. He ran an x-ray that showed she has had numerous mini-strokes. She was very unhappy living with us. We got in contact with some lawyers that could help us get her on Medicaid so we could get her in a nursing home. There was plenty of paperwork to fill out.

While DeAnn was still living with us, we wanted to go to our property out west. Stacy would stay with DeAnn here at my house. DeAnn really liked Stacy and I left them the keys to my car so they could go shopping if they wanted to and go to church.

We went on a hunting trip during the Thanksgiving Holidays in 2006 and took all three of our grandchildren with us. We let Summer go out hunting with Hugh and she bagged her first deer. It was a 6 point white-tail buck. This was the happiest girl in the world, to hear her speak about this deer, it was one for the record books. She asked her Paw-Paw to have it mounted, and of course he did. Summer was ten years old and shot it with an open site rifle. I killed a 10 point white-tail buck; this was the biggest buck that I had ever bagged.

Then one day the lawyers called and said DeAnn had to be in a nursing home now. I found a nursing home that would take her with Medicaid pending. We put her in the nursing home and she did not like it at first. Once she settled in, you could not get her out of there. She has made friends and enjoyed being there.

13

Since I have rededicated my life to the Lord Jesus Christ and my Lord and Savior my life has changed dramatically. My marriage is much better, we do not argue any more, and I am more secure in our marriage. I have witnessed a miracle, a God sent miracle. When we had visited the Second Baptist Church in Highlands to witness our son's baptism a man at the church went into cardiac arrest. Hugh checked on him, his pulse was very weak and he was extremely cold. A call was placed to 911. Then all of a sudden the man collapsed, again Hugh checked his vital signs and there was none. Hugh and a lady began CPR. While CPR was being administered the whole church body began to pray. After about three cycles of CPR the man came back to life and was talking. Shortly afterwards the ambulance arrived to take him to the hospital. Come to find out afterwards, the ambulance was dispatched first to the wrong church. This to me was God's way of letting everyone know that He wanted to take credit for this man's recovery. He did not need any help from the emergency medical personnel. We found out that the man, Sidney was kept at the hospital for observation. The hospital could not find any problems with him; they could not detect any sign of him even having a heart attack. God completely healed him. After all, He is the Great Physician.

I had to change doctors because Dr. Wren was no longer accepting my insurance. I am now seeing Dr. Holm. He left my medication the same except he added a different sleeping medication.

In summation, the lights I saw during the abortion were the Gates to Heaven and God told me that was where my daughter Emily Rose is now living in His grace.

After praying one night, I felt Jesus tell me to tell my story.

The next day Satan showed up demanding I do this and I told him this is a house of God and he needs to leave. I noticed after he left on my right arm up near my shoulder on the inside were fang marks. The night before my next door neighbor had come over to see how I was because I had taken several injections in my back. The next day, we were all outside and I hollered at her and she told me there was a snake underneath her trailer. She has a travel trailer. I told Hugh, so he went to find it and it was a 4 foot water moccasin and Hugh killed it.

One Sunday, Hugh had to work so I went to church by myself. Everything was going along fine on the way home, I was talking with Jesus when all of a sudden I could feel the engine start to miss. I had the car on cruise control set on 65mph. I looked down and I was going 66 mph, I hit the brake and then Satan floorboards the accelerator. I hit the brakes to keep it on 61 mph. Then comes my turn off and after the turn he would not let the car go but 9 mph. I had the radio on a Christian station and I turned it up very loud and I said get behind me Satan, you only like men, you don't like God, I love God, I love Jesus, I love God, I love Jesus. He released the car when someone else was coming up behind me. The car could only go 45 mph. Our car was broke and had to be fixed. We know a mechanic and he doesn't charge us that much for labor. The total cost of parts and labor was $150.

For a very long time I have prayed for God to heal my Bipolar Disorder and relieve me from the pain and anguish of my mental illness. I truly believe that I have received God's grace. I recently learned that my liver is not functioning normally and I can no longer take my psychotic medication. To me, this is a sign from God that He has answered my prayers. All the glory and praise goes to God. God is still in the business of healing.

My husband and I continue to be the best Christians that we can be. My husband just recently told me that he has a calling to be in the ministry for the Lord Jesus Christ. I see him witnessing to our neighbors. With faithfulness and the help of the Lord Jesus we will continue serving the Lord Jesus Christ for the rest of our lives.

I now feel that Jesus is telling me that I am a blessed woman.

978-0-595-48455-3
0-595-48455-7

www.ingramcontent.com/pod-product-compliance
Lightning Source LLC
Chambersburg PA
CBHW020353290526
45785CB00005B/2271